KOREAN ART—1

Traditional KOREAN ART

Traditional KOREAN ART

Edited by
the Korean National Commission for
UNESCO

The Si-sa-yong-o-sa Publishers, Inc., Korea
Pace International Research, Inc., U.S.A.

Published simultaneously in KOREA and the UNITED STATES

KOREA EDITION
First printing 1983
The Si-sa-yong-o-sa Publishers, Inc.
5-3 Kwanchol-dong, Chongno-ku
Seoul 110, Korea

U.S. EDITION
First printing 1983
Pace International Research, Inc.
Tide Avenue, Falcon Cove
P.O. Box 51, Arch Cape
Oregon 97102, U.S.A.

ISBN: 0-89209-014-6

This series is a co-publication by The Si-sa-yong-o-sa Publishers, Inc.
and The International Communication Foundation.

Foreword

The Korean people are artistic, expressing their innermost being in pottery, painting, poetry, drama, music and dance. To most foreigners familiar with Chinese and Japanese art, Korean art comes as a profound revelation and a delightful experience. Korean art differs from the strong, bold aspects of continental Chinese art and from the dazzling colours of Japanese art. Its basic characteristic is simplicity, reinforced by the atmosphere of quiet and serenity which it creates.

Following the publication of *Modern Korean Short Stories*, the Korean National Commission for UNESCO embarked upon a new project, dedicated to seeking real character of Korean culture. This new series deals with various aspects of Korean culture—language, thought, fine arts, music, dance, theatre and cinema, etc. It concentrates on baring the roots of the Korean cultural tradition and demonstrating the process of its transformation. It is hoped in this way to reveal the framework of traditional thought which is fundamental to any understanding of Korea's past and present.

Profound thanks are due to the writers of the individual articles and to the generous sponsorship of the Si-sa-yong-o-sa Publishers, Inc., who once again have turned a dream into a reality. This series, edited by the Korean National Commission for UNESCO, is published by the Si-sa-yong-o-sa Publishers, Inc., in commemoration of the thirtieth anniversary of the Korean National Commission for UNESCO.

Bong Shik Park
Secretary-General
The Korean National Commission
for UNESCO

Contents

Traditional KOREAN ART

Philosophies and Styles in Korean Art

— *A Prelude to the History of Korean Art* —

KIM WŎN-YONG

Art and Art History

Man defines art as what is expressive of his experiences, sensations and mental images, such as painting, literature, dance and acting. The basic factor of art is communication of emotions and, in this connection, Jerome Stolnitz states that when an artist's feeling is transferred to a viewer or listener it becomes art.[1]

In a painting, an artist materializes his sensations in a unified manner by means of line, color and form. His actual work depends on his imagination and the result of his work must be endowed with formal harmony.

A work of art is a new, independent work of unity. It is something that is created. In other words, a thing becomes a work of art only when it is created by man. A landscape, however beautiful, is not a work of art. Similarly, ink splashed on the wall or a dog's paw marks on a piece of paper cannot become a work of art. We respect an artist for his creative power. Hegel asserts that the creation of beauty in art is made possible only by an inspiration.[2]

A work of art, however individualistic, retains something of the social and cultural background in which it is made. Art cannot be maintained or supported by a few artists totally separated from the society to which they belong. Art, therefore, is inseparable from geographic condition, a common tendency and a style. It pulsates within this social framework.[3]

The essential quality of art is beauty; art does not exist without beauty. Then what is beauty? In short, beauty is something pleasant to hear and look at. George Santayana defines beauty as pleasure and contends that a thing cannot be beautiful if it does not give us a feeling of pleasure.[4]

Where does this sense of pleasure derive from? Herbert Read claims that "the sense of pleasurable relations is the sense of beauty; the opposite sense is the sense of ugliness."[5] He states that beauty is a unity or harmony of formal relations among our sense-perceptions. As Santayana says, therefore, beauty is not a perceived fact but a value, sensation or emotion.

Beauty is a sensation based on a harmonized unity or unified harmony. Then why does harmony give us a pleasurable feeling?

I consider that man's favorable response to harmony is rooted in his instinct for preservation of life.[6]

Woman's body is soft and curvilinear. God made woman for man to feel beauty and sexual desire. A female bird is often seduced by the flamboyant colors of a male bird's feathers, and flowers exude fragrance to attract bees and butterflies. Such fragrance and brilliant colors give us pleasurable feelings. Being more sophisticated, man feels from the softness and curvilinear beauty of woman's body a sense of peace, beauty and vitality. What is soft and curvilinear does not do harm to man. Man bleeds when something sharp pricks his body, but something soft and curvilinear gives a peaceful feeling and it is therefore pleasurable.

Man sees innumerable composite units. Of all things, however, man seems to feel the most beautiful unified harmony of harmonized unity in the sense of peace and equilibrium that woman's body possesses.

Any form of beauty man perceives is a harmonized unity that does not threaten life, a peaceful and realistic unity that evokes affection. After all, affection is a physical desire, a form of biological instinct.

Man also sets esthetic standards in natural environments. Children, for instance, find flowers beautiful, and adults enjoy viewing landscape paintings. F. Silbey was right when he said that adjective terms of beauty cannot be made understood without a background of nature.[7]

Beauty, in conclusion, is a sensation empirically formed through natural phenomena related to man's life.

Artist and Artisan

Although all men possess an instinctive esthetic sense, they do not feel it to the same degree.

The qualities of esthetic sense vary according to each individual, each locality and each race. They can be nurtured by education or under the influence of individuals. The refined esthetic sense may be called taste. The development of taste results in the birth of a sophisticated cultural class, a class in pursuit of beauty. Cultured men of this class reflect their esthetic tastes in their clothings and living space. Their life-style may be defined as "mŏt," a Korean word for refined taste. Men of this class are art patrons that constitute a driving force for artistic activities. Paris and New York exist as art centers or artists' Meccas because the populations of these cities are dominated by such cultured individuals and groups. Schapiro calls this class "rentier."[8]

But these people do not create art, for a work of art cannot be produced by esthetic sense alone. An expression of sensation requires methods and techniques that can be developed through training. One can teach or learn how to do, but one can never teach or learn what to do. It is for this reason that Hegel said only those with inborn gifts alone can create a work of art. Here lies the difference between an artist and artisan or craftsman. An artist is able to create a work of art independently. He knows what and how to create it.

Meanwhile, an artisan makes reproductions within an established framework of norm. There is a difference between a painter of art and a painter of signboards, as there is a difference between a sculptor and a stone cutter.

Style and Form

Fine art is a genre of arts. It is a visual art. It is an artist's expression of his imagination in line, color and form, and as long as it is a work of art it must contain beauty.

Architecture, painting and sculpture are classified as major arts and pottery, metal crafts and textile dyeing on other crafts are classified as minor arts.

When an artist creates a work, it has some individual characteristics in terms of material and technique.

A certain painter, for instance, favors pointed mountain peaks on yellow paper and this conspicuous tendency in the way of expression is called style. Style is of technical nature and differs from form which is of common nature. Form can be a result of style, and it is possible that there is "a painting of Picasso form rendered in a Picasso style." Generally speaking, however, form is closely related to shape.

Naturalism and Idealism

Artists work hard in pursuit of their individualistic styles. However individualistic in appearance, their styles derive consciously or unconsciously, from social conditions and cultural traditions to which they belong. If a style of totally heterogeneous character is created, therefore, it does not remain in existence if society does not accept it.

So there are different styles, such as regional, racial, periodic or universal styles. Broadly speaking, styles of naturalism and idealism tend to repeat themselves throughout history.

Let me consider in this context the naturalism of the

palaeolithic age, the idealism that prevailed between the neolithic age and the iron age, the naturalism of the classical period, the idealism of the Middle Ages, the naturalism of the Renaissance period, and the idealism of the 20th century. The repetition of these two broad styles can be traced in Asia as well: the idealism that prevailed through the Yin, Chou and Han dynasties, the naturalism of the Sui and T'ang dynasties in China, the idealism of Arabic world, the naturalism of India, the idealism of Japan and the naturalism of Korea.

An artist of naturalistic style adopts and develops a naturalistic pattern in shape, composition and effect. His standard of beauty is based on Nature. Therefore his style becomes realistic rather than abstract. Outstanding examples of this style are Roman figure sculptures, sculptures of the Sŏkkuram Grotto Temple in Kyŏngju, and landscape paintings of the Northern Sung Dynasty.

A reproduction of a natural scene, however, is not a work of art if it is devoid of an artist's subjective feeling.

Contrary to a naturalist, an artist of idealism perceives objects with his subjective feelings and materializes images, forms and compositions as he sees and feels. They reject the established values of composition and even tend to express almost insane fantasies, such as those of abstractism, cubism or surrealism. He chooses his objects freely, sometimes deforms them, conventionalizes them or schematizes them. Sometimes he expresses his sensations with signs, forms, and geometric patterns.

Character of Art History

What does the science of art history aim at? Art history is a science that deals with art works of individuals, regions, races and mankind. It is to discover styles, schools, and date periods to which they belong. It deals with origins, developments, degeneration and relations of various arts as well as historical significances. A student of art history must analyze esthetic qualities of an art work and the artist's philosophical background as well. Art history is not to do with criticism or appreciation of art. It is a mistake to confuse art history with an act of praise of an individual or a country.

A study of art history of a country may require a study of the history of a specific people. But one must deal with art history with theories and methods used in the study of art history. If specific historical prejudices and views are involved in the study of art history, it fails to become an objective art history. It becomes disqualified as art history; it remains propaganda. In this context, we should warn ourselves against a chauvinistic prejudice and exaggeration in the study of our own art lest it should eventually hurt ourselves.

Art History and Archaeology

There is a problem arising from the relation between art history and archeology. Materials and data for the study of these two sciences are partially overlapped, and they are often called collectively "art and archaeology." In some situations, a student is not certain whether he is a student of archeology or a student of art history.

But these two sciences must be clearly distinguished in terms of purposes and methods of study. While an art historian's objects are only artists and their works, an archeologist's sources of study cover a greater scope such as all the natural remains, dwellings and their environments related to man's activities as well as art objects and other relics produced and used by men. In short, art objects are only a small portion of materials dealt with in archeology. Archeology is made up of prehistoric archeology and historic archeology. Prehistoric archeology, according to a school of contemporary archeology is aimed at restoring and discovering the history of culture, life-style of past men and laws of culture.[9] When an archeologist finds it necessary to study an art object in the process of his archeological study, he must apprehend it only as part of man's cultural activities. He must rely on an art historian as regards the historical understanding of the art object itself.

Characteristics of Korean Art

Anyone who has some knowledge of Asian art can easily discern Korean art from Japanese or Chinese art. But it is not easy to explain the difference in concrete terms point by point.

In his recent research, Prof. D. Seckel defines "Koreaness" by detecting:

1. The decomposition of form-complexes into small elements like a mosaic work.

2. Flat in volume and graphically linear in surface design.

Nevertheless, the underlying characteristics of Korean art, he concludes, are vitality, spontaneity and unconcern for technical perfection (nonchalance).[10]

Seckel finds the first tendency, breaking up designs in a mosaic manner, in details of Punch'ŏng (Mishima) vessels and a lacquerd box, whereas he detects the second tendency in the illustrations decorating the surface of bronze bells, and in a bell dating from the Koryŏ dynasty (918-1392). In the case of the latter, the tendency of rendering pictorial designs in a flat plane tends to deteriorate, compared with the preceding Silla period in which bells were ornamented with flying angels and arabesque patterns in deep relief with sculptural effects. This tendency shows some kind of nonchalance.

Neolithic Korean pottery is decorated with geometric patterns. Since it is not a painted pottery, such incised geometric pattern could be the only way of decoration. But the neolithic pottery was gradually replaced by plain pottery of the Bronze Age.

The linear designs on Korean prehistoric bronzes derive from Sibero-Manchurian bronzes.

Impressed lattice patterns were applied on Kimhae pottery

for some time under a Chinese influence, but this type of pottery was replaced soon by the undecorated Silla pottery.

Linear designs were in fashion in the Old Silla pottery produced in Kyŏngju in the 5th century, but the pottery of other areas in Kyŏngsang Province and those of Koguryŏ and Paekche were devoid of any decoration. The urns made in the Kyŏngju area during the Unified Silla period (668-918) were decorated with stamped designs under a new influence of the art of T'ang China and Persia. But this style of decoration was applied exclusively on urns and other stoneware vessels remained free from any decoration.

Koryŏ celadon vessels were often decorated with realistic designs of flowers and grass. They were also inlaid with pictorial designs. We find an obvious deterioration in inlay techniques and qualities of celadon glaze in the vessels made in the period from the end of the Koryŏ dynasty through the beginning of the Yi dynasty. A method of decorating the whole surface with repeated designs was adopted in the late Koryŏ period. But this method was not used in the white porcelain ware in underglaze blue of the Yi period, and persistent in the porcelain of the Yi period was a return to the rejection of decoration and love of empty space.

This tendency is not of a temporary nature but a consistent one prevailing in Korean art.

There is an opposing point of view conflicting with that of Prof. Seckel who notes a tendency in Korean art of depicting a solid object in a flat plane. In Asian art, there is a tendency to avoid nudity. An artist executes a man's figure with his clothes on. Sometimes a dress is more emphasized than a body. The drapery of a Buddhist image, for instance, covers his entire body. It generally falls in a soft line and spreads out in elegant folds, creating a graceful pictorial effect. This linear tradition[11] is also a basic factor in the Buddhist sculpture of China where a naked body and an uncovered torso were also rendered under an influence of Indian sculpture during the so-called second phase. But the linear tradition was revived soon.

A similar interest in an uncovered torso is also reflected in Korea, for instance, in the gilt-bronze image of Maitreya of the early 7th century in which the torso is entirely uncovered, and in the 8th century images at the Sŏkkuram Grotto Temple. But the flat rendering and linear tradition with emphasis on frontality was revived soon.

This linear tradition in China and Korea is due not to an interest in abstraction or deformation of a body but to an interest in the visual effect of the drapery or dress.

Details of my observation in this aspect may conflict with Seckel's, but I hold no opposing views against his assertion that Korean art is characterized by vitality, spontaneity and unconcern for technical perfection. This characterization of Korean art is valid but remains still vague. More analytical studies from a new angle are required to support the theory.

In fact, a similar characterization of Korean art was already made over a period of decades by other specialists, though there is a slightly varying view according to each individual. Let us consider now the observations of other specialists.

Savory Taste

Muneyoshi Yanagi, an enthusiastic Japanese connoisseur of Korean art, has most passionately insisted on spontaneity as the main characteristic of Korean art. In his book titled "Chosen to Sono Geijutsu" (Korean and her Art) published in 1922, he observes that the beauty of Yi pottery is a beauty that antecedes a concept of what is beautiful or ugly. "It(the beauty) is not made by man but endowed by nature," he contends. "It is born as a result of Korean potters' complete trust in nature, of their freedom from a worldly ambition for human perfection." After all, this nonchalance that Yanagi sees as a virtue seems to accord with what Seckel means by spontaneity. Yanagi's esthetic concept of Korean art and crafts revealed in the book represents the esthetic eyes of ancient Japanese tea masters who adopted crude-looking Yi vessels as their finest tea bowls. This feeling is shared not only by the Japanese but by everybody today.

Ko Yu-sŏp is basically of the same opinion, as he defines the characteristics of Korean art as the qualities of "technique without technique," "planning without planning," "asymmetry," and "nonchalance." "In most cases, a work of Korean art is probably not meticulous in tiny details," he observes. "It rather tends to embrace a wholeness, hence its savory taste in total effect. This nonchalance lies in the docile state of mind of Korean artists and artisans who love nature as it is."[12]

Toyotaro Tanaka, another Japanese specialist in Korean pottery, states that Korean ware is rather born than made. "There is no inkling of hesitation on the part of the potter,"[13] he adds. He also refers this point of view to spontaneity as an outstanding trait of Korean art.

Evelyn McCune, an American art historian born in Korea, asserts that refinement and crudeness are the two polarizing qualities existing in Korean art. Both qualities, she states, reveal honesty and contribute to strength, or vitality.[14] Here the honesty is purity, a trust in nature. According to R. Griffing, Korean art is solid, straightforward and modest and there is no sign of the classicism of Chinese intellects nor the technicality of the Japanese.[15]

Softness, Modesty, Calmness

These interpretations by a number of scholars can in the long run be summed up in Seckel's terms—vitality, spontaneity and unconcern for technical perfection.

Vitality is a strength resulting from the nonchalance of a creator who is free from hesitation, free from the conflict between the beautiful and the ugly. The strength is even enhanced as he reduces decorations and makes the best of the virtue of his material itself, the texture and natural grain, for example, in the case of wood. This tendency is closely related, in the end, to the second and third virtues that we have often discussed, spontaneity and unconcern for technical perfection.

Spontaneity is dual in nature. It involves an artist's attitude toward his work as well as his taste for a spontaneous quality. This love of spontaneity, for instance, is reflected in the tendency of leaving pottery undecorated in Korean art. An undecorated object elicits a delightful feeling of expanded space leading to the lack of artificial pretense. Korean art also tends to be devoid of a feeling of movement and this reflects dislike of disturbance, deformation and convention.

The third and last virtue in question, unconcern for technical perfection, is revealed in Korean artisans' use of warped pieces of wood as beams, pillars and brackets in building a house. It is also reflected in a slightly deformed, crudely glazed bowl Ko Yu-sŏp claims that the savory taste of Korean ware comes from such qualities. St. G. M. Gompertz, an English specialist and collector, explains: "The Korean potters were often careless or inexpert in technique: they were more concerned to achieve an artistic effect and seldom paid attention to detail."

After all, this unconcern is closely related to spontaneity and docile adaptation in natural environments. It is not of fraudulent nature. There is honesty in it. An artisan uses a deformed piece of wood as a beam only when it can fully support the roof.

Silence, Resignation, Enlightenment—Optimism

As we have already discussed, Korean art has been characterized by submissiveness to and love of nature, lack of artificial consciousness. Thus it has developed within the framework of naturalism. Naturalism as such is a vague term. To make it more precise, the Koreans' basic philosophy lies not in a man-oriented idealism but in a naturalism oriented by nature.

Then where and how have such characters of Korean art

been formed? They have certainly come from national character motivated by historical environment.

The Koreans have lived in mild natural environments of a temperate region endowed with the distinct four seasons. This natural condition led the northern nomadic tribes to become farmers as they settled in the Korean peninsula, where they established one of the three cultural areas in the Far East. The peninsula features mountains occupying four-fifths of the total area, mountains of modest height and round peaks that make picturesque landscapes.

It is evident that such peaceful and beautiful natural surroundings nurtured love of nature in the mind of Koreans.

Let us consider the historical background. The peninsula projects from Manchuria and faces the east coast of China across the Yellow Sea. It was a strategic outpost for the so-called Tong-i (Eastern Barbarian) to attack China from sea. Chinese cultural influences penetrated the peninsula with the establishment of Han China's Lolang Colony in B.C. 108. Sandwiched between the northern nomads and Han China, Korea was frequently victimized by foreign invaders. The Koreans were afflicted with sufferings from merciless foreign invaders as well as from utter destitution and political corruption. Amid the sufferings they learned silence and resignation as a realistic solution. Their sense of resignation was not always of a pessimistic nature. It was a means by which to tolerate their hard-pressed reality, a passage to enlightenment and an optimistic philosophy. Accepting and tolerating the hardship, they believed in a fertile land that offered crops honestly.

This historical background seems to have played a great part in the formation of their national traits, such as tolerance of reality, resignation, an optimistic philosophy, naturalness, escapism, and dislike of artificialness. But this reasoning still remains short of what can really support our discussions on the character of Koreans and their art. A more satisfying answer can be found in a careful synthetic consideration of various elements, such as topography, geography, history, cultural environment and life-style, that constitute a specific composite whole.

In conclusion, I am inclined to believe that the cultural tradition of a people derives from a composite mode of life formed over a long period in a specific pattern of environment. Characteristics of art are of course formed by a cultural tradition and they contribute in turn to the formation of a cultural tradition.

NOTES

1. Stolnitz, Jerome, *Aesthetics,* MacMillan, 1965. p. 43.
2. Tillman, F.S. Cahan ed., *Philosophy of Art and Aesthetics,* Harper and Row, 1969, pp. 207–208. Paek Ki-su: *Yesulhak Kaeron* (Outline of Aesthetics), Tongmin Munhwa-sa, 1974. p. 36.
3. Schapiro M. "The Social Bases of Art" in D. Schapiro ed., *Social Realism — Art as a Weapon,* Frederick Ungar, 1973. p. 118, 123.
4. Santayana, G., *The Sense of Beauty,* Modern Library, 1955, p. 51.
5. Read, H., *The Meaning of Modern Art,* Pelican Book, 1950. p. 16.
6. Kim Wŏn-yong: *Hankuk Miŭi T'amgu* (The Beauty of Korean Art), Yolhwadang, 1978, pp. 7–9.
7. Silbey, F., *Aesthetic Concepts,* F. Tillman et al. ed. p. 594.
8. M. Schapiro op. cit. p. 123.
9. Binford, S.L. Binford ed. *New Perspectives in Archaeology,* Aldine Co. 1968, pp. 6–7.
10. Seckel, D., "Some Characteristics of Korean Art", *Oriental Art* XXIII, Spring, 1977. pp. 52–61.
11. Willets, W., *Chinese Art,* Pelican Book, 1958. pp. 372–377.
12. Ko Yu-sŏp, "Chosŏn Kodae Misulŭi T'ŭksaek kwa Kŭ Jŏnsŭng Munjae" (Characteristics of Korean Art), in his *Hankuk Misulsa, Mihak Non-Ko* (Essays on History of Korean Art and Esthetics) T'ongmun-gwan, 1163. pp. 6–8.
13. Tanaka, Toyotarō, *Richō Tōjihu* (Yi Ceramics), Tokyo, 1944, pp. 257–8.
14. McCune, E., *The Arts of Korea,* Tuttle Co. 1962. p. 20.
15. Asia House Gallery, *The Art of the Korean Potter,* The Asia Society, 1968, p. 13.
16. Gompertz G., *Korean Celadon,* Faber, 1963. p. 2.

Some Aspects of the Interrelation of Korean, Chinese and Japanese Arts

KIM WŎN-YONG

The art of China, Korea and Japan share common traits and may form one East Asian art, but they are not one and the same art. There were times when particular fields of art developed an international style among the three nations, but throughout the ages, arts of Korea and Japan maintained national styles and identity despite their outward adherence to Chinese art. It was only Buddhism that established an international art in East Asia based on a common doctrine and canon for two centuries from about 500 to 700 A.D. After the decline of Buddhism, there existed no major driving force or centripetal power strong enough to pull together and promote arts of the three nations as a unity. As Sherman Lee pointed out in his *A History of Far Eastern Art* (1964), Asia is not one, but many, and it is a collection of peoples, of geographic areas and, finally, of cultures. (p. 18)

This paper surveys some aspects of the interrelation among the three national arts based on the above viewpoint.

Prehistoric Art

The fisher-hunters of neolithic Korea came into indirect cultural contacts with northern Chinese farmers only in its third and last stage, during the second millennium B.C., and the painted pottery of northern China managed to leave some traits on later comb-pattern pottery in northern Korea. Nevertheless, the comb pottery retained its tradition almost in full and remained as the main, dominant pottery type until the end of the neolithic period.

As for Japan, minor influences and counterinfluences were exchanged between potteries of northern Kyushu and those of southern Korea across the strait, but the cultural contacts were rather superficial leaving little effects upon their counterparts. A basic difference in trend between Korea and Japan is clearly recognized by the flat, graphic effect of the Korean motif and the Japanese emphasis on plasticity in their neolithic potteries.

During the ensuing Bronze age, the Tungusic population of Liaoning province of north-eastern China and the Korean peninsula developed a distinctive bronze culture of northern lineage characterized by special types of mirror and dagger as well as other ceremonial objects featuring geometric linear patterns and bell devices. The Korean bronze culture strongly affected the cultures of western Japan with the northern Kyushu as its bridgehead. It was due to a large scale immigration of Korean Tungus into Japan, the first wave of major population flow from Korean peninsula into Japan from around 300 B.C. to 700 A.D.

The picture during the prehistoric period which shows little cultural contacts between the Korean peninsula and China may have been due to the differences in subsistence type that prevented major population traffic across the ethnic borderline.

In 108 B.C., Han China established Lolang colony in northwestern Korea as a defensive measure against Hsiungnu of the Mongolian plateau. Han China regarded the Korean peninsula as the left arm of the Hsiungnu. It was, however, this establishment of a Chinese colony that became the decisive moment for the arrival in Korea of intensive and direct cultural impacts from China. South Koreans by then had become sedentary farmers and they were thus ready to receive Chinese culture based on a similar economy.

Sculpture

Buddhism spread into Korea from China toward the end of the fourth century and thence it went into Japan in the mid-sixth century. Chinese Buddhistic sculpture was naturally the starting point for Korean sculptures, and styles corresponding to the so-called II phase (Northern Wei-Lungmen style), III phase (Ch'i-Chu-Hsiangt'angshan style) and IV phase (T'ang-T'ienlungshan style) were reflected respectively in Korean Buddhistic images. Koguryŏ naturally showed strong adherence to the Northern Wei style although the characteristic elongated face of the latter was soon changed to a round type creating a much softer and humane effect. Paekche images were basically in the Wei tradition, but the sensuous modelling of a graceful body doubtlessly reflects influences from sculptures of the Southern Dynasties of China.

It was Paekche sculptors who produced totally Koreanized Maitreyas with unsurpassed physical beauty and spiritual quality around 600 A.D.

Paekche sculptors also worked in the Asuka-period Japan and the famous sculptor Tori who made the Tori Triad of Horyuji temple in Nara was a grandson of a Paekche immigrant. The bronze Triad, however, manifests an undeniable native approach such as seen in the stern face with thick lips and large almond-shaped eyes. Nara-period Japanese Bodhisattvas (7, 8th century) are marked by more Japanized spherical faces with unique childish expression. This return to native approach or style in Japan is the same in the case of Korea, but the tendency is more speedy and intensive in Japan.

The certain vulgarness of plump, even a bit erotic images of the T'ang period was eliminated in sculptures of the Unified Silla period as demonstrated by the images of the Sŏkkuram cave temple in Kyŏngju, but, in the Nara-Heian period (8th-10th centuries) Japan, the T'ang plumpness was pushed a step farther to a bulging, fat body draped in an ample garment with schematized drapery folds. The austere face of a Buddhistic image with—shaped mouth of Nara-period Japan is typically Japanese in effect, a tradition already established in the Asuka period.

Chinese Buddhistic sculpture remained as the source of inspiration and stimuli for Korean and Japanese sculptures until around 700, but thereafter, Chinese sculpture became impotent like Buddhism itself. And, Korean sculpture could not generate a self-propelling force of its own to evolve by itself. In Japan, too, after the manneristic Fujiwara sculpture from the 10th to 12th centuries, a short period of vitality returned at the beginning of the Kamakura period (13th-14th centuries), but Japanese Buddhistic sculpture became virtually nonexistent after the close of the period.

Buddhism itself had come to an end in a substantial sense.

Painting

Tomb painting of Koguryŏ was inspired by its Chinese counterpart, the Han Dynasty. At first, the theme of Koguryŏ paintings was portraits of the dead couple with strict frontality like the Chinese models. Judging from the facial type and brush strokes, paintings of the initial stage in the fourth and early fifth century, appear to have been done by Chinese residents of the former Lolang colony. The painting, however, soon changed to a Koguryŏ style both in its brush work and composition. The dead couple remain as the central theme, but they are now engaged in some sort of activities such as receiving guests or outdoor hunting. Compared to Chinese painting, a Koguryŏ composition is far less crowded and lacks the rhythmic mellowness and dynamism of the former.

Tomb painting was also practiced in north-western Kyushu, Japan, during the sixth century apparently under influence from Korea. The stone-built burial chamber itself was a plan imported from Korea. But, the Kyushu paintings are abstract in essence consisting of mystic symbols and conventionalized human figures. Here again, it is apparent that a strong nationalistic character moved in as soon as the foreign impact reached Japan. This tendency of a quick return to national character in Japanese art seems to be due to geographical isolation and rather a distinct natural environment that forced foreign elements toward speedy adjustment.

In central Japan, the now-destroyed murals at Horyuji temple and those of Takamatsu-zuka tomb, both of Nara, testify that a school or schools familiar with T'ang and even Indian painting were operating in the Japanese capital toward the end of the seventh century. Painters of seventh-century Japan were mostly of Koguryŏ origin, and the murals of the Takamatsu-zuka tomb depicting groups of court ladies may have been drawn also by painters of Koguryŏ lineage. The painting, however, is obviously influenced by T'ang painting as is shown in the composition of overlapped figures, sensuous silhouette and the refined color scheme.

Entering the eighth century, however, a national, Japanese school called Yamatoe emerged opening the way for a long, distinct tradition culminating in the Korin style. It should be noted that the establishment of the Yamatoe school roughly coincides with the ceasing of sending official envoys to T'ang by Japan at the end of the ninth century.

The Ma-Hsia school tradition prevailed during the early Yi period (15th-16th centuries), but entering the 17th century, what can be called a Korean school emerged. The new school led by such masters as Chŏng Sŏn (1676-1759), Kim Hong-do (1745-?), etc., took up themes from the daily life of contemporary Koreans with keen interest and sympathy. The painters, both professionals and amateurs alike, also made sketches of actual landscapes which looked more familiar and closer to Koreans than the imaginary, manual-copied landscapes of the early Yi period in the Chinese manner. The new movement in painting coincided with the efforts made by contemporary Yi scholars to improve social conditions and strengthen national identity by promoting practical knowledge rather than studying the metaphysical theories of Confucianism. It was a national reaction against the two foreign invasions around 1600.

Not all of the later Yi painters, however, belonged to the Korean school, and the Wu-school paintings and wen-jen-hua of Ming and Ch'ing were also taken up by many seriously. Nevertheless, painting in the later Yi period was firmly established as Korean painting and it was by no means a regional variant of Chinese painting.

In Japan, the Ma-Hsia school was faithfully followed by Shubun and Sesshu etc., but their paintings are more angular in form and stronger in ink contrast. The Kano school represented by Eitoku (d. 1590) of the 16th century pushed farther the visual effect of the Sesshu style through an emphasis on clear-cut composition with provocative, strong coloring. The Japanese character of Japanese painting reaches the culmination in the sinuous, playful forms, lines and colors of Ukiyoe and romantically decorative paintings such as those of Korin. This is not a departure from Chinese painting, but it is completely an independent national style.

Ceramics

Pottery of the early historical period of Korea remained rather unaffected by Chinese pottery. Thus, Silla pottery, the grey stoneware of southern Korea from around 200 to 600 A.D., is noted for its uniqueness of unglazed texture, incised geometric designs and above all the bold, dynamic silhouette of vessel forms. Tens of thousands of Silla pottery were discovered from tombs, but a brownglazed bottle of Tech'ing kiln of the fifth century is the only Chinese pottery discovered from a Silla tomb (The Tomb of the Heavenly Horse, Kyŏngju). It is only from around the seventh century that Silla potters started applying China-derived lead-glaze and made vessels of the T'ang type such as bottles and covered bowls with a short ring-foot.

On the other hand, however, a large scale immigration of ancient Koreans to central Japan starting from the early fifth century A.D. transplanted Silla pottery *into* Japan where it was called Sueki. The Sueki pottery soon underwent its own evolution in Japan developing stylistic changes, but it remained basically a variant of Silla pottery for about two centuries although the proportional ratio among various vessel forms considerably differs from that in Korea.

Unlike the ancient Koreans of the Three Kingdoms period, however, the Koryŏ (918-1392) potters took up seriously the stimuli from celadon technique of Sung China. The largest centers of Koryŏ celadon are situated at the south-western extremity of the Korean peninsula. Chinese trade ships bound for Korea left the modern port of Ningpo at the mouth of the Yangtze River and crossed the sea directly to reach the south-western tip of Korea. Sometimes, storms brought wrecked trade ships on the shores and local potters might have had chances to personally investigate Chinese celadons with astonishment and admiration. But, the emergence of celadon in Koryŏ may have been the result of actual arrivals of Chinese potters in Korea who must have discovered rich celadon clay in south-western Korea.

Koryŏ celadons of the initial stage of the late 11th and early 12th centuries reflect traits of Chinese celadon, but the next two centuries were a period of self-generated evolution characterized by a unique glaze color, the so-called inlay-technique sporting ornamental designs of Koryŏ origin.

After the fall of Koryŏ, Koryŏ inlaid celadon became the so-called Punch'ŏng ware of the early Yi period (1392-1910). The Punch'ŏng ware, though derived from Koryŏ celadon, is a totally new pottery type in its taste,. technique and in overall effect. It is truly a Korean pottery completely freed from Chinese celadon tradition.

Yi blue-and-white ware is derived from its Ming counterpart, and it adopted some vessel forms and design elements of the latter at the beginning. But, it soon discarded the foreign elements and became a unique ware with strong Korean characteristics. The Japanese Daimyos who invaded Korea at the end of the 16th century took home many Korean potters with them at their retreat, and these potter-prisoners from southern Korea became founders of famous Japanese kilns of porcelain ware still thriving in the Kyushu area. Early pieces made by the Korean potters immediately after their arrival in Japan were Yi type blue-and-white as well as Punch'ŏng ware.

But, they soon started to lose the Yi flavour and became Japanese ware in all aspects according to the historical process of Japanization of foreign elements.

Through the above hasty survey of some aspects of artistic interplay among the three nations, the following points may be concluded.

1) The flow of artistic influences and inspiration has always been one-way traffic from China to Korea or Japan. The vitality of Chinese art as such was due to the fact that China not only received stimuli from India and Central Asia but also had several artistic centers within her own territory which could act as stimulants among themselves. Such external and internal stimuli are essential for development of a national art.

   On the other hand, Korea and Japan could not have more than one powerful art center in their territory, and had to rely on stimuli from without or the rise of particular social groups or classes and sympathetic national sentiment to develop an active art. At the same time, the old value system of East Asian peoples to look upon China as the center of world civilization also contributed greatly to the one way traffic of artistic influences.

2) Korea acted as a cultural bridge between China and Japan, but she was also at times an independent source of

inspiration for Japanese art from the Bronze Age to the seventh century.

3) The three nations have their own national art styles based on different life ways, philosophy and aesthetic senses. Chinese art is characterized by an emphasis on formality, order in complexity, and technical perfection.
   Japanese art is marked by a basic trend of romantic decorativeness and sophistication in visual terms. Korean art, however, is characterized by a consistent approach of optimistic naturalism with preference for simplicity and naivety.
4) A new art form or style was transformed into native styles in a short period probably within several decades, and if a foreign style survived longer, it was due to a large scale immigration of populace like the case of the Sue pottery of Japan.
5) Buddhism gave birth to an art that can be called the Buddhistic art of East Asia from around 500 to 700. When Buddhism lost its role as the basic driving force, international art also dissolved, and the interplay of national arts became occasional, sporadic and intermittent.
6) Korea's strong adherence to Chinese art is due to the geographical and historical background. The Koreans are a Tungusic people affiliated with peoples of Manchuria and Mongolia, and the Korean peninsula has been a sort of a dagger pointed at the side of China. Thus, the ruler of the Chinese mainland must have obtained the consent of Korea, by force or negotiation, to accept it as the administrative apex of the Asian continent. The close relationship between China and Korea, set up since Han China, not only caused the continuous, intensive inflow of Chinese culture into Korea but also elevated the status of Korea to the second most civilized nation in ancient East Asia.

Art Objects from Ancient Tombs

CHIN HONG-SŎP

It was customary in both East and West to bury the dead along with burial objects in a tomb, and many diverse burial objects have been unearthed in Korea. Five gold crowns were discovered in Kyŏngju. Other burial gifts, too many for a single person, were also excavated from Kyŏngju tombs. They include personal ornaments, pottery, bronze, gold and silverware, glassware, armor and weapons, and equestrian equipment. Animal-shaped pottery, especially from Kaya and Kyŏngju area, provide important data from which one can infer the belief and customs of contemporary society. Pottery vessels with incised drawings and attached figurines, also discovered recently in the Kyŏngju area, provide further information on the ancient customs of the Silla dynasty.

The vast quantity of luxurious burial objects was discovered in the Kyŏngju area, thanks mainly to the particular method of tomb building employed at that time. The ancient tombs in this area, called the "cairn with wooden chamber," consist of a box-shaped wooden chamber containing a wooden coffin and burial gifts placed inside a pit. The burial chamber is then covered with a pile of boulders, each the size of a human head, and the entire structure is covered by a huge earth mound. A Silla tomb constructed like this was almost impossible to plunder. Thus, many Silla tombs in the Kyŏngju area were able to preserve burial objects intact.

Tombs of Koguryŏ and Paekche are chamber tombs which permit easy access. Because they have been plundered by tomb robbers of both ancient and modern times, fewer burial objects were discovered in these tombs. Those found are so poorly preserved that it is difficult to speculate about their original state. Consequently it is almost impossible to deduce what the material cultures of Koguryŏ and Paekche were like through the burial objects.

A chance discovery in 1971 of the tomb of King Muryŏng (d.523 A.D.) of Paekche in Songsan-ri, Kongju, yielded an abundance of burial objects of various materials, however.

An ancient tomb in Kyŏngju, subsequently named the Heavenly Horse Tomb, was excavated in 1973. Later Tomb No. 98 in the same area, composed of southern and northern mounds, was excavated. An extensive survey and excavation of the Anapchi Pond in Kyŏngju, which started in 1975, also yielded many diverse art objects including roof tiles, Buddhist images and other metal works.

Burial objects unearthed from these tombs may be classified into several categories: personal ornaments including gold crowns, belts, girdles, armlets, earrings and necklaces;

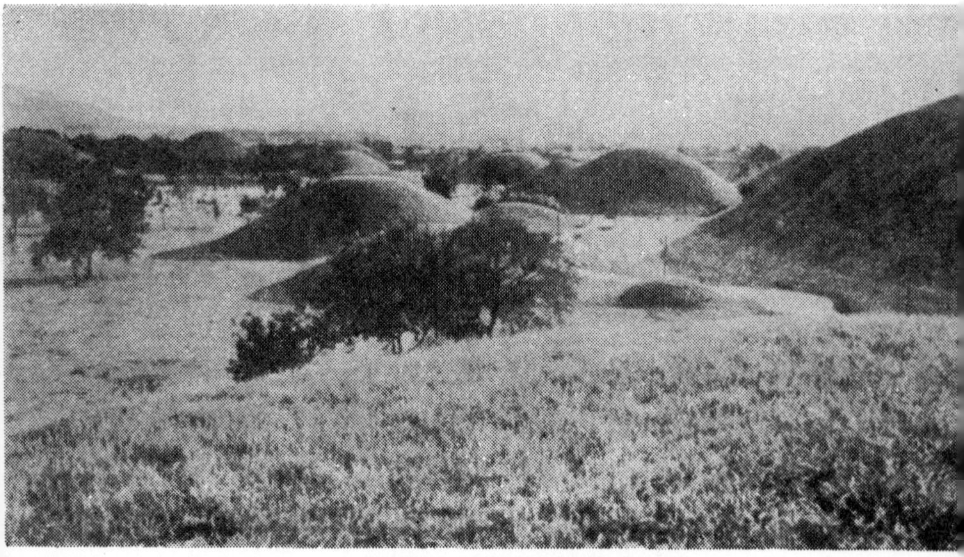

A cluster of ancient tombs, Kyongju

mounted cups made of gold, silver and glass; elegantly shaped pottery in the form of mounted warriors, ducks, horses and boats; pottery with attached human and animal figurines or incised drawings; glass cups and bottles; bronze kettle-ewers called Chiao-tou in Chinese; daggers with inlaid gold mounting and others. Some of the burial objects reflect ancient Korea's cultural exchanges with regions as far west as the Middle East.

So far about ten crowns made of gold and other materials have been unearthed from the Kyŏngju area and two sets of gold ornaments that were attached to royal silk hats have been found in the tomb of King Muryŏng. The gold crowns excavated in the Kyŏngju area are more or less the same type: a circlet made of cut sheet-gold with three tree-shaped uprights in front, flanked by two antler-shaped upright. Innumerable tiny circular gold spangles and comma-shaped jades are attached to the uprights by means of twisted gold wire. Most of the gilt-bronze crowns excavated in this area are similar.

Discovered with these crowns were triangular caps with gold pointed tops. Also attached to each of the caps is a horn-shaped frontal ornament also made of gold. In the case of a tomb in Yangsan, the inner cap was found inside the outer crown, but in other tombs inner caps were discovered outside the coffin, suggesting that inner caps may have been worn separately (as ordinary daily headgear) while the outer crowns were used on special occasions.

In contrast with Silla crowns, which reflect the Shamanism of the Siberian steppes, the head ornaments from the tomb of King Muryŏng of Paekche are decorated with rhythmic patterns of lotus and honeysuckle. In other words, the Paekche pieces are related to Buddhist art of the Six Dynasties period in China.

Girdles and pendants of Silla and Paekche are more or less similar. Girdles usually consist of many metal plaques, a long buckle and a flat thong. Originally the plaques were riveted to a piece of leather or cloth backing, but this material has now completely decayed. Each square plaque or link, as well as the heart-shaped pendant hinged to the plaque, has a conventionalized floral design in openwork. Usually a girdle is accompanied by up to ten or more pendants originally suspended on the girdle. Each of the pendants is comprised of several ovoid plaques hinged together, and an end-finial of various shapes is hinged to the last plaque. Bracelets are decorated with embossed dots, each encasing a tiny jewel. Sometimes the outer surface is simply serrated in the tradition of ribbed-shell bracelets. A pair of silver bracelets from the tomb of King Muryŏng are decorated with twisting dragons in relief. They bear inside an inscription indicating the name of the artist and the date of making (520 A.D.). According to the inscription, the bracelets were ordered and worn by the Queen. A vast quantity of comma-shaped jade-pendants with gold caps was also, discovered in the tomb of King Muryŏng, along with many gold floral spangles that once adorned the royal robes of King and Queen Muryŏng.

A mounted cup, or a shallow bowl on a tall stem, is the most popular and abundant vessel in Silla pottery. There are,

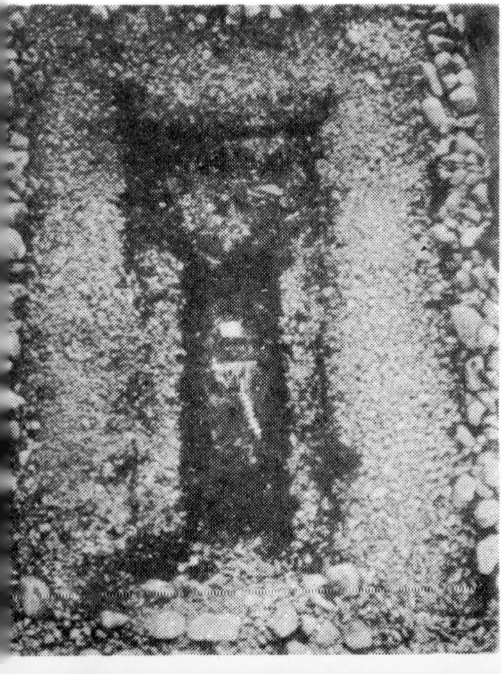

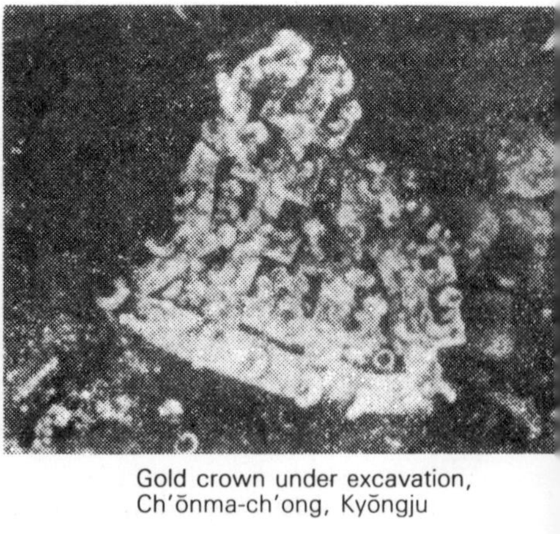

Gold crown under excavation, Ch'ŏnma-ch'ong, Kyŏngju

Excavation of Hwangnam-dae-ch'ong's wooden coffin

however, mounted gold and silver cups like the ones from the Gold Crown Tomb and Tomb No. 98 in Kyŏngju.

Sets of glassware were found in the Gold Bell Tomb, the Gold Crown Tomb, the Heavenly Horse Tomb and Tomb No. 98, all in Kyŏngju. There is a controversy, however, over their places of origin, and it is highly likely that not all of them are local products. A glass ewer from Tomb No. 98, for example, seems to be a late Roman glass, probably imported through China.

A silver cup excavated from Tomb No. 98 is outstanding in its rich embossed design of mythical animals within hexagonal frames. Similar designs decorate the soles of gilt-bronze shoes from a tomb in Kyŏngju, and the design and technique are apparently derived from Sassanian art.

Three bronze mirrors from the tomb of King Muryŏng are valuable specimens of the Three Kingdoms period. The mirrors are copied after Chinese mirrors of the Six Dynasties. The one that bears an animal-band design in addition to the familiar longevity prayer is identical in size and decoration to one from the Kannon-zuka Tomb in Takasaki, Japan. They must have been cast from the same mold in Paekche.

Every Silla tomb produces a vast amount of pottery, often kept in a separate pit used for burial items. Silla pottery is a hard grey pottery without glaze. Its shape, texture, and simple, incised linear decorations are unique to Silla pottery, which is characteristically stark and spontaneous. There are pieces, however, with human and animal figurines attached to the shoulder. A jar with a long neck discovered in a Kyŏngju tomb is particularly striking in its applied decoration—a group of human figures including a copulating couple. These vessels with applied figurines are no doubt ceremonial utensils like the elegantly shaped pottery mentioned above.

During the seventh century, glazed pottery appeared for the first time in Korea. The glaze is the brownish green lead glaze, but the three-colored *San-ts'ai* also exist, although in a limited number.

It is difficult to cover every aspect of the art objects recovered from the tombs of the Three Kingdoms period in this brief introduction, but hopefully the richness of the excavated material has been demonstrated.

Structure of Ancient Tombs

The Three Kingdoms each show their own characteristics in tomb structure. The unique external form of the stone or mounded Koguryŏ tombs cannot be found in the tombs of Paekche or Silla. The Koguryŏ people used granite or marble to construct large chambers underground. Especially remarkable is that they recreated ground structures in the subterranean chambers of such tombs as Ssangyŏng-ch'ŏng, Ch'ŏnwangjisin-ch'ong and Anak Tomb No. 3.

The tombs of Paekche, on the other hand, are commonplace structures comprising round mounds. Their interior consists of an oblong stone chamber connected to the outside through a long corridor and affixed with a drainage channel. This is certainly different from the style of Koguryŏ tombs. In addition, some Paekche tombs are made of bricks, another feature that cannot be found in either Koguryŏ or Silla tombs.

On the other hand, Silla tombs maintain a special variety of twin-mound shaped like a gourd. A Silla tomb contains a huge wooden box with the coffin inside buried in a stack of stones, a peculiar style that cannot be found in Koguryŏ or Paekche tombs. The unique structure of the tombs shows the peculiar conditions that existed during the Three Kingdoms. The tomb of King Muryŏng of Paekche, the Ch'ŏnma-ch'ong (Heavenly Horse Tomb) and Hwangnam-dae-ch'ong (Tomb No. 98) of Silla, all excavated recently, not only showed characteristic structures unique to the two kingdoms, but provided large quantities of relics which had been kept intact, thereby furnishing valuable new materials on the ancient art and culture of Korea.

The Tomb of King Muryŏng (d. 523 A.D.) was originally regarded simply as one among a cluster of old tombs scattered in Songsan-ri, Kongju. A brick tomb that had already been opened stands in front of the royal tomb, but at first nobody thought the mound behind it to be a tomb at all, much less the tomb of the great King Muryŏng of Paekche. The structure of the royal tomb consists of a main chamber and a frontal passage attached to the south wall. Both the main chamber and the passage are shaped like a tunnel and are built with shard ornamental grey bricks. The main chamber is 4.2m long (N-S) and 2.9m wide (E-W) with a height of 2.9m.

The emergence of brick-built, tunnel-shaped tombs in Kongju, the second capital of Paekche from 475 to 538 A.D., was due to a direct influence from Liang China, with whom Paekche had maintained close political and cultural relationships. The lotus pattern depicted on the bricks in relief was copied after a Liang model. There are five onion-shaped

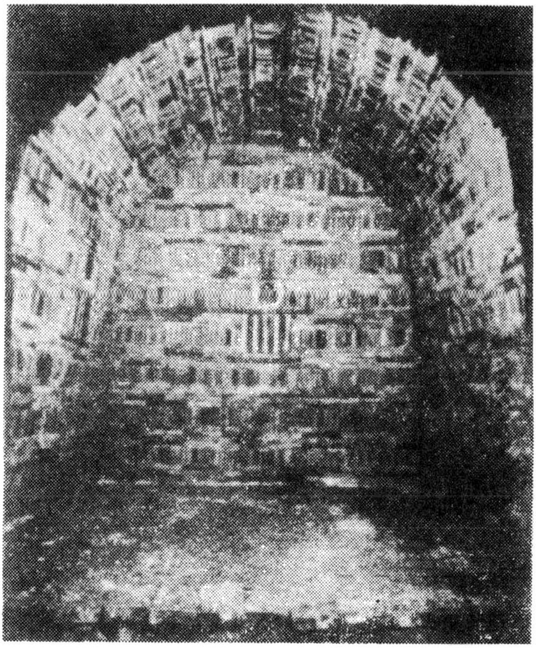

Interior of King Muryŏng's Tomb, Kongju

niches on the walls—two each on the east and west walls and one on the north wall. A porcelain oil-lamp with a burnt wick stuck to its mouth-rim was placed in each niche, suggesting that the lamps had been left burning when the tomb was sealed after burial.

The space where the coffins of the King and Queen were placed side by side with their heads pointing to the south is elevated. Unlike a Silla tomb, which contains many burial items, a limited number of offerings—a pottery bottle and several bronzes and porcelain wine cups—were placed in the lowered space. A bronze mirror and personal ornaments were also placed toward the northern end of the chamber.

Two porcelain jars imported from China, bronze wine cups, and a stone unicorn were placed in the middle of the entrance passage as a guardian in the Chinese fashion. Two stone plaques inscribed with a brief account of the royal funeral were placed in front of the unicorn. According to this inscription the king died in 523 and the queen in 526.

The inner structure of a typical Silla tomb in the Kyŏngju area is a box-shaped wooden chamber. This was protected by a mound of river boulder and a huge earth mound. A single coffin was put inside the chamber, which was placed either inside a subterranean pit or above the ground. The head of a dead person in a Silla tomb always pointed to the east. Two or three shelves were made on the east wall, or a special chest was placed between the east wall and the coffin to store various burial goods. In some cases, an additional square pit was provided for a large number of pottery vessels and other burial goods. As time passed, the ceiling of the chamber decayed, and the stones above would fall in to crush everything from the coffin to the burial goods. This fact made Silla tombs an impossible target for tomb robbers. It was an expensive system, however, because the very structure of the tomb did not permit the placing of a second coffin in the chamber. Thus when the spouse died, they had to construct a new tomb. The occasional gourd-shaped mounds were actually tombs of a couple constructed side by side. In early Silla tombs, however, burial pits of the members of the same family shared a single common mound.

The mound of the Ch'ŏnma-ch'ong, or the Heavenly Horse Tomb, in Kyŏngju rises 12.7m high above the ground with a diameter of 51 to 60m. Excavation and reconstruction have determined that the wooden burial chamber was originally 6.6m (E-W) × 4.2m (N-S) with a height of 2.1m. It contained a lacquered wooden coffin measuring 2.15 × 0.8m. A man, apparently a member of the royal family, in full attire with a magnificent gold crown and gold girdle lay in an extended posture within.

A "treasure box" toward the east wall contained a rich variety of burial goods. Above iron kettles in the bottom of the chest were various vessels of gold, glass, pottery and lacquer. Three saddles were on the top tier, beneath pairs of birch bark mudguards. A heavenly horse painted in white pigment on each of the side-panels of the mudguards gives the tomb its name.

The largest Silla tomb of the gourd type is the Hwangnam-dae-ch'ong, or Hwangnam-dong Tomb No. 98. The tomb has a height of 22.2m and a diameter of 80m. The overall length of the twin mound is 120m. The two rows of post holes around the inner stone mound are a peculiar feature of this tomb, which dates from the fifth century A.D. Since the wooden chamber was placed above the ground, unlike the usual tombs with dug-in pits, a scaffolding-like timber frame must have been necessary to hold the protective stone walls around the wooden chamber.

The wife of the man interred in the south mound was buried in the north mound. The lady wore a gold crown, a gold girdle, five pairs of gold bracelets, gold rings and gold earrings. Her robe, though now decayed, was once bedecked with gold ornaments. Her husband's tomb contained an additional pit to store a huge cache of iron weapons and tools and pottery. He wore a gilt-bronze crown and a gold girdle with fewer ornaments. He had in his treasure several glass vessels, including a spouted bottle with single handle which must have been imported from the Middle East via China. The broken handle of the bottle had been wound with gold thread.

The Origin of Korean Sculpture

CHIN HONG-SŎP

The origin of Korean sculpture can be traced back to the clay figures and vessels in the form of horses and riders on cylinders from Three Kingdom period tombs. But they show very little sculptural quality and technique unlike contemporary China, which produced fine works at a much earlier date. It was the introduction of Buddhism which first stimulated the true sculptural spirit in the peninsula.

Images of Buddha were needed to spread the faith; they were made first in Koguryŏ during the latter half of the fourth century. From this Koreans developed their whole art of Korean Buddhist sculpture. Since Buddhism, however, was an imported religion through Chinese interpretation, this early sculpture had no relation to primitive handicraft of the Korean people but was an imitation of the Chinese technique, and took some time to arrive at perfection. Also more time was needed to achieve a typical Korean expression both in skill as well as in faith. The form of the Buddhist figures of the early period therefore shows strong Chinese influence and this trend continued even after the Unification, though from this time onward a typically Korean style and technique emerged from assimilation and digestion of the foreign influences.

n addition, some non-Buddhist sculpture survives from the early Buddhist period. Of these the steles and protective stone works deserve attention. They contain the figures of civil and military officials set in front of tombs, stone lions, twelve horary gods (the signs of the zodiac) in relief around them, and memorial steles with the tortoise base and dragon capitals. But the development of these figures shows a close relation to that of Buddhist sculpture.

The sculptures so far considered were made of clay, gold, gilt bronze, iron, bronze or stone. Superb examples remain in all these materials, but many of the metal objects have been badly damaged. Among the extant examples are some remarkable pieces of stone carving, scattered about the hills and fields of the country, astonishing us by their quality as well as their number. Many of them are made from the abundant and excellent white granite; its qualities contributed to the development of sculptural skill.

Buddhist Sculpture

We have seen that Buddhist sculpture began in the second half of the fourth century with the coming of Buddhism to Koguryŏ. But extant works all date from the end of the Three Kingdoms period or later. So we have no knowledge of the earlier works but presume them to be imitations of Chinese style. A tiny seated gilt bronze Buddha, only five centimeters high, found near Seoul in 1959, was certainly a Chinese work made about A.D. 400, and suggests that Chinese forms were the model for early Korean work.

Nevertheless Korean Buddhist sculpture between the Three Kingdoms period and the Yi dynasty period shows its own development in skill and style. This development was partly due to outside influence and partly due to the peculiar history of Korean Buddhism. Thus we can distinguish the types of the Three Kingdoms, Unified Silla, Koryŏ, and Yi dynasty periods. The distinctive features of Buddhist images in each period will be our subject.

Buddhist images of the Three Kingdoms period have much in common, but slight differences can be found in each kingdom. A small number of figures (gilt bronze or clay) from

Koguryŏ, like other plastic work, are characterized by boldness and vigour in representation. But the forms of the extant images, seeming to have been made in the sixth century, are still in the tradition of Northern Wei, modified by the influence of the northern Chi-chou (550-577) style by plump stubby figures and the full face of the main image. Despite Chinese influence we can appreciate the typical Koguryŏ style from the chiselling of the robes and the (more simple) petals of the pedestal.

On the other hand, Paekche Buddhist images have survived in much larger number than those of Koguryŏ. Most of the extant figures were discovered in the region of Puyŏ. Whether made of gilt bronze or stone, they all have more or less the characteristics of the Chinese style. Besides they do not differ from Koguryŏ sculptures in any major respect. But they all seem to have a gentle grace, which is typical of Paekche. The modelling of the figures and robes is basically similar to Koguryŏ work, but the lotus petals, the naturalistic disposition of the drapery and the way the weight of the body seems to be thrown on to one leg, are Paekche features.

All these Paekche images show a gentle style and expression. Of these the gilt bronze half-seated Maitreya coming out of the seventh century is an outstanding work among Korean gilt bronze figures; its influence spread to Japan. Even by that time Paekche style does not seem to have been fully developed.

The written records of Silla are far more detailed than those of Koguryŏ and Paekche, and include much information about sculpture. However, Buddhism came late to Silla, and was not active until the first half of the sixth century, so that we know little of Buddhist sculpture before the second half of the same century. Therefore the extant works made of materials such as gilt bronze or stone must have been produced in later years. Some of these figures are outstanding examples of the half-seated form. Although they show Six Dynasties tradition and a considerable influence from Chi-chou (in the pose and the arrangement of the robes and drapery), the half-seated stone

Bodhisattva from Ponghwa shows the confidence of the sculptor which puts it in the first rank of Oriental sculptural masterpieces.

Besides the stone trinity from the Kyŏngju region, known as "the baby Buddhas", with its slightly girlish appearance, short bodies and childish faces, gives a strong impression of Chi-chou influence. Probably the finest one among the old Silla gilt bronze figures is the head of the gilt bronze Bodhisattva found on site of Hwangnyong-sa. The outline of the face and the expression show a complete assimilation of Northern Wei and Chi-chou styles indicating highly developed faith as well as great skill.

When Silla united the Three Kingdoms it combined all their sculptural styles with a new fashion coming in from T'ang China to develop a distinct style of its own, marking advances in both power and delicacy at the same time. This spiritual and technical progress reflects the country's new confidence. The most important works of this period are made of stone, gilt-bronze, gold and iron. However, the style of Unified Silla had not matured completely by the middle of the 8th century but through the transitional form at the turn of the seventh and eighth centuries finally developed in the course of the eighth century into the perfection of the Sŏkkuram Carvings. The sculptures are characterized by two main streams: one is an effort to achieve the delineation of bodily lines rather than a feeling of grandeur, the other gives the impression of a buxom female figure, thereby presenting a sharp contrast to the products of the early Unified era, which shows influences from the Six Dynasties (China), Indian and Paekchean styles.

In these masterpieces spiritual values and technical skill are in perfect harmony, the bodies are realistic, yet of transcendental beauty. Although influenced by high T'ang style, they are not mere imitations of it but a perfect assimilation of that style by Silla sculptors, which became a model for subsequent Silla work.

But after the period of Silla's peak prosperity such sculpture began to decline. The casting of iron Buddhist images infused a fresh spirit into decaying Silla sculpture. From the ninth century onward iron figures became popular in Silla with a tendency towards asymmetrical and schematic forms and drapery, which profoundly influenced the iron sculptures of the following Koryŏ period.

The Koryŏ dynasty continued the Silla policy of encouraging Buddhism. As the faith flourished, so sculpture continued. Above all, Koryŏ sculpture was influenced by two factors: the vigor of the new dynasty and the popularity of the Dhyana (Meditation) school. The former became manifest through the large scale of early Koryŏ stone and iron figures, the latter in the rapid decline in formal excellence. However a few of the images, belonging to the early period, preserve some traits of late Silla and a feeling of solidity. But they show the Koryŏ qualities in the schematization of the robes and the technique of the head. Of these qualities the technique of the head, heavily emphasizing the face, is common in almost all figures of the Koryŏ period and especially the seated stone Bodhisattva at Taehŭng temple. In addition we have large numbers of other extant images made of stone, iron and gilt bronze, etc. But only a few have any merit. Thus we see that the Koryŏ figures began by continuing the Silla tradition, but soon developed new features without an entirely new style. Asymmetrical disposition of the limbs and weird facial expression caused the loss of spiritual beauty. And from the reign of military officials the Dhyana school resumed its power and those trends were accelerated, yet they represent the special characteristics of the period.

With the beginning of the Yi dynasty, Buddhism suffered from political oppression and quickly declined. Buddhist art of Koryŏ with its too plump body and splendidly heavy form declined rapidly: the modelling of the figures became unnatural, far removed from the real human form; the drapery became highly formalized and the figures entirely static. Nevertheless, a few early Yi dynasty figures deserve notice particularly the lacquer or wooden figures.

Non-Buddhist Sculpture

In addition to Buddhist sculpture, we should consider the non-Buddhist sculptures of tomb sites or temples. From the tortoise base of the stele for King Muyŏl, Unified Silla, there is a continuous tradition through Koryŏ to the Yi dynasty. These contain military and civilian officials in stone in front of the tombs, stone lions around them, the twelve horary gods carved in relief around the base of tombs, pagodas and stone lanterns. Of these, tortoise stele-pedestals and the horary gods have been accepted in Buddhist art and we must not exclude them.

Most of these funerary sculptures that remain have a known date of erection and since the development of their styles can be traced they are of great importance to art historians. But the tomb-carvings are much less common than Buddhist images and the main stream must be sought through the temple images.

The first military and civilian officials in stone appeared in the early period of Unified Silla, although partially damaged. Both of the figures in this period are set up at either side (in rows), the military figure is dressed in armor and carries weapons, while the civilian is wearing ordinary clothes and has his hands joined in front of him. Among these are a military official foreign to Silla in type, with what the Chinese would have called a barbarian face. Here we can see some Western influence. This custom continued through the following periods, but the figures grew less naturalistic, the armor and robes became stylized, the faces expressionless and the style heavy and dull, so that no individual works deserve special mention.

Stone lions were not only placed at royal tombs, but were much used in Buddhist buildings and were placed around the stone pagodas. They are set in each of the four corners or in front of the tomb at some distance. The poses of the lions differ. Of these the lion of the Tabo-t'ap at Pulguk-sa is superb in the technique of its carving. The Silla custom of setting stone lions in front of tombs was continued later by putting various kinds of stone animals in front of Koryŏ and Yi tombs. The stone tigers, horses and sheep set in rows on either side before the later tombs lend splendor to the precincts, but unhappily this splendor is not conveyed in the technique of their sculpture. They are static and debased works.

The series of twelve animals corresponding to the signs of the zodiac and originally used in the measuring of time, were used from Latter Han times onward as symbols of the points of the compass. From T'ang times they were used as protective figures around tombs. In Buddhism they became the twelve spirit warriors of Bhaisjyaguru, and appear frequently in Buddhist art. In Korea they were first depicted in relief on stone slabs around tombs in Unified Silla and continued until the Yi dynasty. The tomb of Sŏngdŏk alone has three-dimensional figures: standing men with animal heads, dressed in civilian clothes but holding weapons. The reliefs gradually deteriorated in quality as time passed; the representation was simplified and lost vitality. The forms of the figures also changed in later periods. In Koryŏ times the standing figures with animal heads of Silla stood full-faced with animal headdresses; in Yi Period the figures had animal bodies. Furthermore the relief became very shallow as well as much smaller and eventually they were replaced by Chinese characters.

From the Three Kingdoms on, steles were set up; after the unification of the peninsula the stele resting on the back of a tortoise, with a dragon coiled on the top of the stele, became common. Of these the stele of King Muyŏl's tomb is the first known in the later, more elaborate style. The head of the tortoise is shown in life-like fashion and the carapace was realistically marked with vigorous patterning. The capital shows six dragons, in a style of rounded sculpture derived from

China, with realistically powerful heads and scales. But in later times of Silla the tortoise began to have a dragon-like head unlike the pattern of the conventionalized carapace. This type of tortoise pedestal continued to be used until Koryŏ times when the animal became even more fantastic and no longer resembled the living reptile.

On the other hand the dragon capital slowly changed from a rippling to a three arched form, and retained its life-like appearance to early Koryŏ times, although with gradual decline into mediocrity.

While in a conventional way masks would not be regarded as sculpture, the wooden masks of Hahoe deserve to be included. Most Korean masks, made of gourds or paper, were customarily destroyed after being used in one play and very few old ones survived. The survival of the Hahoe masks made in late Koryŏ or early Yi days is due partly to the fact that they were carved from wood, and partly to the religious veneration with which the villagers regarded them. They are true folk products, unaffected by sophisticated culture, and inspired by the simple but ironic wit of country people. They were used in a masked drama which gave a satirical account of aristocratic society, so they are comic, and even insulting to the persons they depict. Furthermore they are all heavily painted and achieve broad visual effects.

This general account of Korean sculpture shows that the art was originally stimulated by the Buddhist religion, and since Buddhism was imported from China it was at first strongly influenced by Chinese art. During the Three Kingdoms period, sculptural types of Northern Wei, Chi-chou and Sui were copied with little adaptation, in spite of minor differences in each of the three Korean kingdoms. A distinctively Korean style developed, together with an assured technique, after Silla had united the peninsula. Indeed, the best works of Unified Silla have a place among the world's masterpieces. The middle of the eighth century was Silla's golden age of sculpture, and the gradual decline thereafter was never arrested. Later periods have their own features which closely reflect the vicissitudes of Korean Buddhism. Among the many fine examples of non-Buddhist sculpture, tomb sculptures are very noteworthy. Their development seems to be in close relation to that of Buddhist sculpture.

The finest works of Korean sculpture were produced when the Buddhist culture of the country was at a peak. So the art declined as the role of Buddhism in the general culture became less important. From the beginning of the Yi dynasty a policy of oppression of Buddhism and admiration of Chinese art led to a neglect of sculpture which finally ended in a stylistic decline that lasted until the end of the dynasty.

Ancient Korean Art and Buddhism

HWANG SU-YŎNG

Korean art has undergone many transformations during its long history—a history as long as that of the people who created it. It was in later years that the Korean people settled on what is called the Korean peninsula; before that the stage of their activities extended over the expansive Asian continent, undergoing migrations and state-building for a considerably long period. Finally they gave birth to three states on the Korean peninsula and in Manchuria about the time of the dawn of the Christian Era. It was also about that time that the prototype of Korean art took shape.

Needless to say, the stone age and the metal age preceded the triangular emergence of the Three Kingdoms—a field of research for archaeology. The technique of producing and employing iron implements had inseparable relations with the growth of state power. As artifacts representing this age we may cite ritual utensils and arms, which show the origin of the beauty and skill of Korean art. However, these metal tools are not the only artifacts showing the origin of Korean art. Painted pottery and the sculpture of animals on a rock found in March 1972 near Pangudae along the lower stream of a river in Onyang-myŏn, Ulsan County, South Kyŏngsang Province, are priceless relics which also illustrate the origin of Korean painting and sculpture.

The remaining artistic relics which were produced before

the Three Kingdoms period or early in that period are very few in number. Therefore I will omit that part of Korean art which belongs to the category of primitive art and concentrate on the period from the fifth century onwards when Korean art started to achieve real development, believing that the introduction of Buddhism was a decisive factor in its development. This, however, does not mean that I intentionally slight various complex elements which Chinese culture brought to ancient Korean art prior to the introduction of Buddhism.

Compared with the original elements mentioned above, the influence of Buddhism on Korean art was doubtless far more dominant and colorful. Meeting the requirements of a world religion, Buddhism spread in all Oriental countries, including China. In view of the route by which Buddhism was introduced, it should be noted that the religion brought with it elements from India and from the land west of China, in addition to Chinese elements. Buddhism introduced not only its extensive and profound philosophy but the art which accompanied it, thereby giving an impetus to the traditional basis of art in the Orient.

The Three Kingdoms were no exception; and the Buddhism which reached the Korean peninsula by land and by sea in the latter half of the fourth century gave to ancient Korean art a stimulus which was unprecedentedly powerful. What I want to emphasize here is that we should not overlook the growth of our ancient states and their original art which enabled them to absorb and digest the alien religion and its art. That is to say, our ancestors had already developed a mature tradition which enabled them to respond to Buddhist art immediately after its introduction. Theirs was not a passive posture; rather they promptly assimilated the alien elements and availed themselves of the opportunity for enriching their own culture.

How the Three Kingdoms assimilated Buddhist art can be explained by pointing out the facts that the Korean received it not as on blank paper; its advent was not a dominant wave engulfing them but they utilized it as a turning point to develop their own art on the basis of their tradition. The fact that the Korean states could grow to such an extent to assimilate the foreign art form promptly must not be overlooked or ignored. As the Korean kingdoms had already attained a high level of development, Buddhism could enjoy rapid propagation immediately after reaching Korea. Even in Old Silla which was the last among the Three Kingdoms to introduce Buddhism, it showed a remarkable degree of assimilation, as recorded in the statement that "temples thrive as though they were stars in heaven and Buddhist pagodas are everywhere as though they were geese in their migratory flight" by the end of the Three Kingdoms period. The record on the monument of Priest Sat'aek Chijok of Paekche describes one aspect of Buddhist prosperity by saying that "they build temple buildings out of gold and erect pagodas made of gems."

I will now discuss the two fields of Buddhist art which formed the mainstream of ancient Korean art.

First let me deal with ancient Korean architecture. The two oldest wooden buildings extant are Pusŏk-sa in Yŏngju and Pongjŏng-sa in Andong, both in North Kyŏngsang Province, and we have not found wooden buildings older than these. It is expected, however, that future archaeological excavations and inquiries into the traditional style of Korean architecture will reveal many unknown facts about such ancient buildings as government offices, royal palaces, and Buddhist temples. These inquiries should take into account not only the real or imaginable characteristics of each individual building but the arrangement of small and large buildings which formed a compound.

In the case of the Buddhist temple, a prayer hall and a pagoda were constructed in the center of its precincts, the former housing a Buddha image, the latter accommodating a sarira (Buddha's remains), both objects of worship. This layout underwent some transformation as the years passed, but the rule remained fixed throughout the Three Kingdoms period that the main hall stood to the north facing the south, with the pagoda placed in front of it. From the middle part of the seventh century and during the Unified Silla period, the one-pagoda system was split into a two-pagoda layout, one standing in the east and the other in the west in front of the prayer hall.

As one good example of the one-pagoda system we may cite the nine-story wooden pagoda in the Hwangnyong-sa precincts, a work of Old Silla. The two-pagoda system is exemplified by the Pagoda of Sakyamuni and the Pagoda of Tabo (Prabhutaratna) standing in the Pulguk-sa precincts in Kyŏngju, eighth century masterpieces. Though erected in the 17th century, the five-story wooden pagoda in the Pŏpchu-sa in North Ch'ungch'ŏng Province, called P'alsang-jŏn Hall, is not only the only wooden Buddhist pagoda remaining intact but retains the one-pagoda style.

As explained above, the layout of both large and small Buddhist temple grounds followed a fixed form in ancient times. The traditional style dating back to the Three Kingdoms period was observed strictly, at least in the central part of the temple precincts, not only in temples located on flat lands but in those built on mountains in provincial areas, a location which came into vogue in the ninth century, though there were naturally some restrictions coming from topographical features.

It is noteworthy on the other hand that this basic form of layout applied to Buddhist temples was very similar to that of royal palaces. One recent example can be found in Kyŏngbok Palace rebuilt in the latter half of the 19th century. Its main edifice is Kŭnjŏng-jŏn which is surrounded by a corridor rectangular in shape pierced by Kŭnjŏng Gate facing due south in front of the hall. This is strikingly similar to the temple layout in which the prayer hall and the pagoda are surrounded by a corridor, with the inner gate standing in the center of the southern side of the corridor. The layout of Pulguk-sa which was renovated recently is generally similar.

The only difference between temples and palaces is that while the seat of Buddha was installed in the center of the main hall in the former as a symbol of the ruler of the spiritual world, the royal seat was placed in the center in the latter as a symbol of the ruler of the secular world. The affinity between palaces and temples can be explained by the fact that the two were both buildings designed to display authority, while forming the mainstream in ancient Korean architecture.

Compared with wooden buildings, a far greater number of stone pagodas remain today. As products of Buddhist art, stone pagodas came into being in Paekche and Silla around 600 and soon spread to all parts of Korea. They became so abundant in the 10 centuries of Buddhist propagation that Korea was called the "country of stone pagodas." In the three Far Eastern countries believing in Buddhism, China was famous for her brick pagodas and Japan for her wooden pagodas, while Korea won fame for her stone pagodas which are not only unique in terms of materials but peculiar in terms of form. Both Korean and foreign scholars are unanimous in concluding that the style embodied by Korean stone pagodas cannot be rivalled by that of any similar edifices erected in any other Oriental Buddhist country.

Preserving the long tradition of ancient Korean art, our stone pagoda architecture left many masterpieces during the 10 centuries of its development. The multi-storied stone pagoda standing on the ruined site of Mirŭk-sa in Iksan, North Chŏlla Province, still boasts of the oldest and grandest form, true to the record contained in old literature that the pagoda, erected during the reign of Paekche King Mu, is "the best of all the stone pagodas in the East." The three-story stone pagoda in the ruins of Kamun-sa along the eastern coast, built by Silla King Munmu the Great soon after Silla's unification of the Korean peninsula, can be considered typical of Korean stone pagodas. The three-story stone pagoda of Pulguk-sa, built in the mid-eighth century, displays the beautiful harmony of Silla pagodas. Besides these angular and multi-story stone pagodas, we can find some stone pagodas in extraordinary shapes, the best among which is probably the Pagoda of Tabo (Prabhuta-ratna) at Pulguk-sa and the stone pagoda with four lions platform at Hwaŏm-sa in Kurye, South Chŏlla Province.

In the next place, we will turn to Korean sculpture, which had such inseparable relations with Buddhism that it cannot be thought of without referring to the latter. Almost all of our sculptural masterpieces dating as far back as to the ancient period are objects of Buddhist worship, namely, statues of Buddha and Bodhisattvas. In these ancient sculptural works we can trace the transformation of styles in different ages and their deep connection with the contents of faith which saw a shift of emphasis from one aspect to another. In terms of materials each period produced its own masterpieces, whose raw materials ranged from wood to metal and stone. Almost all the ancient sculptures now extant are of metal and stone.

Stone statues, which came into being in Korea in about 600 when the Three Kingdoms period came to a close, occupied a large segment of our ancient sculpture. This can be explained by the fact that Korea produces high-quality stones in every part of the peninsula. Since time immemorial our ancestors have turned their attention to the high-quality stone material which abounded in their land. By giving their full efforts to it, they succeeded in producing excellent stone pagodas and stone statues which form the two greatest pillars in our ancient art. I cannot but point out the heavenly favor accorded our art in terms of raw materials. Although not a few gilt statues were produced in the Three Kingdoms period and later, they are mostly small in size. Not only independent stone statues of large size but those carved on rocky cliffs started to emerge around 600, toward the close of the Three Kingdoms period. A survey conducted after the liberation pinpointed the likely birthplaces of Korean stone sculpture in Paekche and Old Silla, as well as the route by which the art was presumably introduced to the country.

In the case of Paekche the survey indicated that such areas

as Sŏsan and T'ae-an, northwest of Kongju and Puyŏ, were probably the birthplaces of its stone sculpture. Two stone statues of triad with Bodhisattvas, presumably the oldest stone sculptural work of Paekche, were discovered. The discovery led to the conclusion that Buddhist culture came to Paekche by sea and that an advanced culture flourished first in the northwestern part of the kingdom.

It was also concluded that Buddhism reached Old Silla at about the same time by way of Yŏngju and Ponghwa in the northern part of that kingdom. A statue of a seated Buddha carved in a cliff and a statue of a seated Maitreya (Pan-ga and meditation style), both huge works, were discovered in the northern area of the former Silla territory, suggesting that Buddhist culture came to Silla by land. It was also presumed that the northern district occupied a strategic point in terms of traffic and that there were cultural exchanges with Koguryŏ to the north. Moving southward gradually, Buddhism finally penetrated the Silla capital of Kyŏngju. Stone statues representing the first half of the seventh century were discovered mainly along the northern slope of Nam-san (South Mountain) in Kyŏngju. Most representative of these finds is the famous statue of Buddha which was formerly enshrined on Samhwaryŏng Peak on Nam-san and is presently preserved at the Kyŏngju branch of the National Museum.

We can cite two relics which, unlike the Samhwa-ryŏng statue, remain at their original sites. One is a group of statues inside the cave temple of Sinsŏn-sa on Tansŏk Mountain in Sŏ-myŏn, Wŏlsŏng County, produced before the unification of Silla. The other is a group of statues in the Sŏkkuram grotto on Mount T'oham in Kyŏngju, masterpieces of Unified Silla. The two temples were constructed as grottos and part of their original shape still remains. The Sinsŏn-sa cave temple is a natural grotto whose wooden upper structure with a tile roof has been lost. Shaped in a form, the grotto has 10 large and small statues carved in relief on the eastern, southern, and northern walls. Fortunately the cave temple contains an inscription on the southern wall explaining the statues. I visited the cave temple in 1968 and again in 1969. I examined the inscription and discovered the name of the temple and that of its main Buddha. The standing Buddha, measuring 23 *ch'ŏk* in height (one ch'ŏk is about 30 centimeters), and two standing Bodhisattvas, all carved on the innermost three walls, were presumed at the examination to be a statue of Maitreya accompanied by two attendant Bodhisattvas. The seated statue of Bodhisattva in meditation with one leg of Pan-ga (lalita) style, which is replaced beside the main Buddha, is the only one of its kind which is preserved at its original site. That the main Buddha was presumed a Maitreya makes an important suggestion as to the contents of the Buddhist faith in Silla toward the close of the Three Kingdoms period. Another important fact is that this cave temple is presumed to be the one (Central Peak Cave) where General Kim Yu-sin who made the most meritorious contribution to Silla's unification of the Three Kingdoms prayed for the achievement of this great task when he was a young Hwarang. The group of Hwarang General Kim led was called "Yonghwa Hyangdo"; and Yonghwa indicates Maitreya, so that it is apparent that he believed in Maitreya and the object of his worship was a statue of Maitreya. Our ancient Buddhist statues should be understood in their relation to the faith of the age in which they were produced.

The T'oham Mountain grotto is known more widely than the above mentioned older one. Even though we are still insufficiently attentive to this grotto and particularly to its contents, a series of repair projects was carried out on this cave temple in the 1960s, which led to new inquiries. The inquiries, first conducted from the aspects of architecture and sculpture, developed into a project to ascertain the name of the main Buddha and then into an examination of the fact that the main Buddha faces due east, taking into consideration the relations the grotto may have had with other Silla relics along the eastern coastline. One of the most remarkable relics along the coast of the East Sea is the undersea mausoleum of King Munmu the Great who achieved the unification. Discovered in May 1967 by the Five Silla Mountains Survey Team sponsored by the *Hanguk Ilbo* newspaper, the spectacular undersea mausoleum led historians to the inference that Mount T'oham on which the grotto is located had close relations with the East Sea. They advanced the presumption that the primary purpose of constructing Sŏkkuram was to offer prayer to King Munmu's undersea mausoleum in the East Sea toward which its main Buddha looks.

Even though our ancient works do not retain their original shape in most cases, either physically or spiritually, our deep affection for these relics and long research will finally help us determine their true meaning and clarify the true nature of our ancient Buddhist art, thereby restoring our long-severed tradition. The inheritance of the tradition of our ancient art is not an easy task, and it requires long painstaking efforts. During the reign of King Kyŏngdŏk of Silla, who can be compared to King Kongmin of Koryŏ in fondness for art, the famous sculptor Kanggo Naemal produced a copper statue of Yaksa (Bhaisajya-guru) weighing 306,700 *kŭn* (one *kŭn* is about 600 grams) at Punhwang-sa. This also illustrates the long tradition and high-standard of technique of Silla sculpture. The fact should be examined anew that the stone statue and pagoda of Pulguk-sa and Sŏkkuram were produced at the time when the giant metal statue was made. It should also be noted that Silla sculpture reached its apex only 200 years after the introduction of Buddhist art.

So far I have dealt with two divisions of our ancient art—architecture and sculpture. In architecture I discussed stone pagodas in detail, saying that they are the finest of ancient Korean art works. Due to the durability of their material and structure, stone pagodas were able to endure, and one thousand several hundred are still extant. They were so numerous in Korea that country came to be known as the "country of pagodas." Korean pagoda architecture developed its own unique style, which has been inherited throughout the generations. Some foreigners are of the opinion that Korean art is an inferior imitation of Chinese art, and there are even some Koreans who hold the same view. However, that fact remains that an art given brith to and developed by a nation is its own art. While assimilating Buddhism, a world religion, the Far Eastern countries developed their own unique style of pagodas by following their own tradition and reflecting their particular geographical and productive features.

The same can be said of sculpture. Although Korean artists followed the Chinese conventions for sculpture, the mature expression was different from the start. The three Korean kingdoms were different from China in Buddhist faith. For instance, although the belief in Maitreya was the same, it should be emphasized that Korea differed from China in her manner of assimilating it. The belief in Maitreya in Old Silla was ardent because the desire to achieve the national goal of unifying the peninsula. The faith had close relations with the birth of the Hwarang system. The peculiarity of Silla's faith in Maitreya was evident also in the sculpture of Buddhist statues, objects of worship. The faith resulted in the development of Maitreya statues, especially those showing Banks and meditation style in both stone and metal. The above explanation is sufficient to indicate the background of the seated statue of Maitreya meditating with Pan-ga style (lalita') which is one of Korea's most precious national treasures and one of the world's greatest artistic masterpieces.

Ancient masterpieces are all products of mature material and spiritual conditions. At the same time artists required a tradition shaped in the passage of many centuries and a refined technique. In order to renew their tradition, they needed the assimilation of foreign elements ceaselessly. Fortunately, the introduction of foreign elements has never ceased in our history. What counted most was that the Koreans were prepared with their rich tradition for assimilation of foreign influence. It may not be an easy thing to revive our long-severed tradition; but, for that purpose we must conduct research and make painstaking efforts over an extended period of time.

The Pagoda as an Art Form and Object of Faith in the Three Kingdoms Period

HWANG SU-YŎNG

Buddhism, which was introduced to Korea by way of northern China during the latter half of the fourth century, had spread throughout the Korean peninsula by the first half of the sixth century. Of the three kingdoms, the northernmost, Koguryŏ, was the first to accept the Indian religion, followed by Paekche and finally by the southeastern kingdom of Silla which adopted Buddhism about one century after the other two kingdoms did so. Buddhism spread first by land and then by sea. Although Silla was the last kingdom to espouse the new faith she nevertheless had advantages which enabled her to synthesize and develop a Buddhist culture of her own. Geographically, occupying the southeastern corner of the peninsula, Silla was in a better position to preserve her own indigenous culture and at the same time to assimilate a new civilization.

According to historical records, Priest Sundo took Buddhist scriptures and Buddhist figures with him when he first preached Buddhism in Koguryŏ in 427. Records state that three years after that, in the fifth year of Koguryŏ King Sosurim's reign, two Buddhist temples were constructed in the kingdom's capital city: Sŏngmun Temple and Ipulnan Temple. These were the first Buddhist temples built in Korea, but it is unfortunate that their exact sites and size cannot be pinpointed or calculated. However, it is assumed that the two temples were sanctuaries in which Buddhist figures, objects of worship, were enshrined although it is not certain whether or not pagodas were built as part of the temple complexes. All that can be said is that, since the Chinese people at that time worshipped not only Buddha images but also holy relics of Buddha (called *sari*), similar rites were conducted in contemporary Koguryŏ. If relics of Buddha were brought to Korea along with Buddha images, the assumption is that the pagoda, in which relics were enshrined, were erected within the precincts of early temples. It can be said, therefore, that the origin of Korea's art in pagoda construction goes back to early in the Three Kingdoms period when Buddhism first came to Korea. The worship of Buddha images and of his holy relics is believed to have been practiced in all three kingdoms and, if so, it is considered that the three kingdoms also had the same temple construction plan in which the pagoda stands side by side with the main temple. This is the same as the Chinese but different from the Indian plan for temple construction. In India only the pagoda, which enshrines the object of worship, was constructed while Buddha images did not appear until much later.

Thus, the pagoda was built from the first days of the Buddhist mission in Korea. Attesting to this fact is an inscription on a stone monument which records the reason why Paekchean minister, Sadajijok, came to build a temple about the middle of the seventh century. The monument was discovered in the ancient capital of Paekche, Puyŏ, in 1948 and is now preserved in the Puyŏ branch of the National Museum.

Wooden Pagodas

As in the case of China, earlier temples were built by the

state as well as by kings, and pagodas were usually built of wood. This was also true of the later kingdoms, Unified Silla and Koryŏ. That is, since wooden pagodas represented all pagodas in the Korea of that age, their scale cannot be compared with pagodas made of materials other than wood. Unfortunately, no wooden pagodas remain today. Anyway, it can be said that in Korea the wooden pagoda preceded the stone pagoda and its scale gave it a dominant place in the precincts of a temple.

As mentioned previously, no wooden pagoda survives to this day. However, the sites of such pagodas are found in many places, one being discovered in 1938 in a village on the outskirts of P'yŏngyang. The site, determined to be that of Kŭmgang Temple which was built in 498, is on the banks of the Taedong River. An octagonal pedestal in the center of the temple site is presumed to have been the site of an octagonal wooden pagoda. It is very large, its sides measuring 10.02 to 10.23 meters, with a gate to its south and a corridor surrounding it on three sides, east, west and north. It has not been determined how many stories the pagoda had although the site has been ascertained as that of a pagoda due to ancient relics found in its surroundings as well as from literary sources. The fact that the oldest wooden pagoda in the northern part of Korea was octagonal draws special attention because the stone pagodas developed later in this region were octagonal also. This, it is assumed, was due to Chinese influence further to the north.

Next, the situation in Paekche, which occupied the western region of the peninsula, must be considered. Unlike her neighbor to the north, Koguryŏ, Paekche had frequent contacts with China and India by way of sea routes and Buddhist temples in the kingdom were so numerous that history describes Paekche as the "land of temples and pagodas." And it is well known that Paekchean Buddhist art flourished to such a degree that it exerted a profound influence on the art of neighboring Silla and Japan. Unfortunately, only a few of the sites of her wooden pagodas have been confirmed by archaeological excavation although there were once pagodas erected in the precincts of many temples.

When Buddhism was first introduced to Paekche, that kingdom had settled around in Seoul as her first capital. No doubt many temples were built in that area but not even one temple site has been located so far. Kongju was Paekche's second capital and from thence she finally settled in Puyŏ for a capital until she was finally conquered by Silla in 660. It is only in her last capital, Puyŏ, that the sites of a few wooden pagodas are found. Most representative of these is the one located in Kunsuri, Puyŏ, as the result of an archaeological survey conducted in 1936. The pagoda site is square and stands on a north-south line with the main temple building, and both are surrounded by a corridor. The fact that this construction method coincides with that of Shiteno-ji in Osaka, Japan, is proof that there were cultural relations between Japan and Paekche at that time. Two Buddhist figures unearthed from the site, one of stone and the other of a gold-bronze alloy, helped determine the period in which this wooden pagoda was constructed: sometime during the latter half of the sixth century. Another wooden pagoda site, on Mt. Puso in Puyŏ, is smaller than the former. In the autumn of 1964, an archaeological survey team discovered yet another temple site along the Kŭm River and the fact that a wooden pagoda was once there has been confirmed. A small metal pagoda, discovered on the southern slopes of Mt. Kŭmsŏng, Puyŏ, in 1947, is a good example of the style of contemporary wooden pagodas and a valuable relic with which to review the art of building during the Three Kingdoms period. It is a one-story square pagoda and its parapet and detail are exquisitely executed.

Lastly, official recognition of Buddhism was long delayed in Silla as compared with the other two kingdoms. However, records concerning the construction of Buddhist temples are comparatively many. The oldest recorded temple is Hŭngyun Temple which took 17 years to build (527-544) and it is recorded a wooden pagoda was constructed in the temple precincts. According to ancient records, the Silla people made it a practice to offer prayers from February 8 through 15 while walking around this pagoda.

More famous and larger than this pagoda was the 9-story wooden pagoda which once stood in the precincts of Hwangnyong (Yellow Dragon) Temple in Kyŏngju, which is said to have been the largest and best pagoda in the Three Kingdoms. It was so called because, according to legend, after King Chinhŭng ordered a new palace be built on the eastern side of the royal palace, he saw a yellow dragon ascend to heaven from the very spot on which the palace was to be built and so instead he ordered that a temple be constructed on the site. The temple took 13 years to complete (552-566) and its companion wooden pagoda was completed in 645, 80 years later, during the reign of Queen Sŏndŏk. The following story is recorded concerning its construction.

High Priest Chajang of Silla while on a trip to China, it is said, received an oracle in a dream from a god-man who told him that if a 9-story pagoda were built in the precincts of Hwangnyong Temple, the state would live in peace. Upon his return home, he recommended that the queen build the pagoda at the temple and the queen summoned her ministers for consultation. The ministers, in turn, recommended the queen to invite master artisans from Paekche since it was an impossible project for Silla alone. Silla requested Paekche to send a team of artisans in exchange for treasure and so a Paekchean master artisan named Abiji came to Silla with 200 artisans to construct the pagoda. And following is related concerning the construction of the pagoda.

Paekchean master artisan Abiji dreamed that he saw his homeland vanquished the night before he was to erect the central pillar of the pagoda. Work stopped. Then suddenly there was an earthquake and he saw an old priest and a Herculean giant come through the main gate of the temple and set the pillar in place. Seeing this he was even more fearful and so he completed the pagoda. The pagoda enshrined one hundred holy relics High Priest Chajang brought home with him. The completed pagoda is about 225 feet in height.

Hwangnyong Temple was protected by the state and considered by the people as one of the treasures of the kingdom. Each of its nine stories was given a special mission to guard the kingdom and the people. The pagoda, standing in the center of the capital, presided over the destiny of the kingdom. The fact that this pagoda was burnt to the ground five times and each time was reconstructed, twice by Silla and three times by Koryŏ, is primarily due to the significance the people attached to it and the worship people offered to this national monument. The site survives today in Kuhwang-ni in Kyŏngju, at which can still be seen the 49 large foundation stones from which the size of this pagoda has been determined.

Stone Pagodas

As explained above, wooden pagodas were the vogue during the peak of the Three Kingdoms period, but during its closing years stone pagodas appeared in Paekche and then in Silla. Stone pagodas were built because they were considered more durable and easier to build than the larger wooden pagodas, which cost much more than stone pagodas and more vulnerable to destructive forces. Good quality granite stone is found in abundance in the areas of ancient Paekche and Silla. Using stones as material, the two kingdoms attempted to manufacture their own art works and objects of worship using techniques developed in their experiments in construction with wooden materials. It was not confined to building stone pagodas, but stone works came to occupy an important place in the history of Korean art as is seen in stone lanterns and

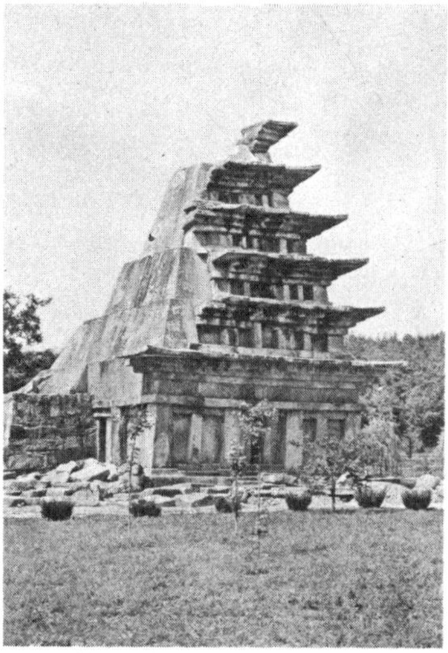

A multi-storied stone pagoda at the site of Mirŭk Temple, Iksan.

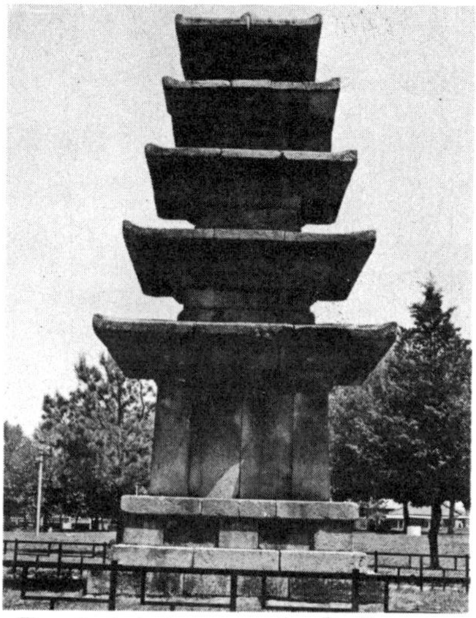

Five-storied stone pagoda, Puyŏ.

stone figures of Buddha.

The first stone pagoda was erected in the kingdom of Paekche because of the fact that Paekche developed the highest degree of sculptural art among the Three Kingdoms during the period her capital was at Puyŏ (538-660) and this is confirmed by the fact that the oldest stone pagoda extant stands on a temple site at Iksan, 25 miles from Puyŏ. Only two of Paekche's stone pagodas are still extant although the temples they were part of have long gone. Of the two multi-story pagodas, the one on the site of Mirŭk Temple is older than the other in view of its style and it is the largest granite pagoda in the Orient. At present only six stories of this square pagoda remain although it is assumed that it originally had seven or even nine stories.

It is easily discerned that this pagoda resembles the wooden pagoda in style, that is, it is a translation into stone work of the wooden pagoda style once in vogue in Paekche. The first story, measuring three *kan* (One *kan* is equivalent to 1.88 meters) wide, has a gate on each of its four sides. The roof of each story has wide eaves as is the case with wooden pagodas. Opinions differ as to when this pagoda was constructed, but from its style and literature related to it, this pagoda can be reasonably estimated to have been built around the first half of the seventh century.

The multi-story pagoda stands south of Puyŏ on what has been confirmed as the site of Chongnim Temple. It is smaller than the former and from its second story up its scale gradually dwindles up to the fifth story. The stories are so regularly piled one upon another that it looks simple, but here simplicity yields a rhythmic beauty. Close scrutiny of form and detail reveals that it is also patterned after the wooden pagoda, but in comparison with the multi-story pagoda at Mirŭk Temple some variations in artistic form are noticed. Inscriptions carved in 660, the year Paekche was vanquished, are found on the four sides of its first story. These inscriptions led scholars to believe falsely that this pagoda was erected to commemorate the victory of the T'ang Chinese general who commanded the T'ang expeditionary forces. However, later archaeological surveys confirmed that it was a pagoda built in the precincts of an ancient temple. It is believed to have been built sometime during the first half of the seventh century, later than the one at Mirŭk Temple in consideration of its style. With these two stone pagodas still extant, it can be said that Paekche started constructing stone pagodas early in the seventh century. Korea's stone pagodas originated from these two, the oldest in Korea. From then on many stone pagodas were constructed around the country, indeed so many neighboring countries called Korea "the land of pagodas."

On the other hand, the development of Silla stone pagodas has different aspects from that of Paekche, although Silla started building stone pagodas almost at the same time. Silla's oldest stone pagoda at Punhwang Temple in Kyŏngju is estimated to have been built in 634, during the reign of Queen

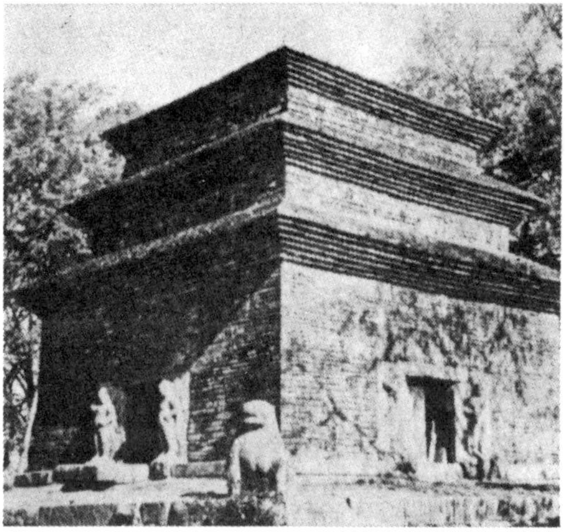

Three-storied stone pagoda at the site of Punhwang Temple, Kyŏngju.

Sŏndŏk. This stone pagoda is so built that it almost looks as if it were built of brick. However, the material used is not brick but stone cut small and rectangular like the form of a brick. It is constructed by the method used for brick pagodas. Because of its peculiar style and because it is made of stone by methods used in the construction of brick pagodas, it is the oldest and the only Silla pagoda extant today. This pagoda is very precious for the study of Korea's pagodas although only three of its stories remain. A stone casket, discovered in its second story in 1915, contained many precious relics, including glass beads and gold and metal artifacts.

As explained above the stone pagoda was first built in the western and eastern regions of the Korean peninsula during the first half of the seventh century according to styles peculiar to each region. Their peculiarities, it is believed, were derived from the different architectural styles of the kingdoms of the times and from their relations with different foreign countries. Paekche's highly-developed architectural art can be seen from the historical fact that Silla invited Paekchean artisans to build the wooden pagoda at Hwangnyong Temple, and its art no doubt had a strong influence on later developments in the construction of stone pagodas. On the other hand, Silla delayed for about one hundred years before accepting Buddhism and in the earlier part of her history she came under the strong influence of Koguryŏ, while the influence of the Northern Dynasties of China came to Koguryŏ down the peninsula. The earlier brick pagodas Silla built are still found around Andong. The brick pagoda obviously had its origin in China, although the art did not flourish on the Korean peninsula as it did in China. In Korea the brick was replaced by stone.

The two styles of the pagoda construction developed by the two southern kingdoms of Korea in their earlier history were finally sythesized into a style unique to the Unified Silla period. This synthesis is considered impossible unless the Three Kingdoms had been unified by Silla; this great historic event was realized in 660. Hereafter, Paekche's stone pagoda patterned after her wooden pagoda was united with the Silla style, which was patterned after the style of her brick pagoda, and the fusion of the peculiarities of styles were synthesized to produce a style unique to the Unified Silla period. Stone pagodas having this unique style of a new age are those now found on the sites of Kamŭn Temple and Kosŏn Temple outside Kyŏngju, both built immediately after Silla unified the Three Kingdoms, that is, during the latter half of the seventh century. The former, built by King Munmu who accomplished the unification of the Three Kingdoms, can be said to have embodied the greatness of the age, the person and the state which combined to produce the pagoda. Because of this fact, the stone pagoda, as a work of art and not an accumulation of lifeless stones, represents the history and art of the time and conveys the technical feats and the objects of worship to posterity.

Regrettably, it seems the kingdom of Koguryŏ fell before she could start building stone pagodas. This may be explained by the fact that, since she bordered China to the north, she was too occupied with her own defense against the incursions of the northern tribes to give time to developing the art of constructing stone pagodas. In fact, after Koguryŏ moved her capital to what is now P'yŏngyang, she fought such unified continental powers as T'ang and Sui. At the same time she was not geographically endowed, like her southern neighbor Paekche, to develop the Buddhist arts fully. Also, during her declining years she held Taoism in higher regard than she did Buddhism and for this reason some Buddhist priests fled from Koguryŏ to Paekche. These are some reasons, if not all the reasons, why Koguryŏ failed to develop her own style of stone pagoda construction. An ancient literature records that an octagonal, seven-storied stone pagoda once stood in the vicinity of Yongt'ap Temple in P'yŏngyang, but no clues remain concerning the location of the site. Also, history records a three-storied stone pagoda, called the Pagoda of King Ayuk, stood within Liaotung Fortress, but again this is difficult to believe.

In the above, pagodas built during the Three Kingdoms period following the introduction of Buddhism to Korea have been considered in respect to the materials used in their construction. Large wooden pagodas were built by all of the Three Kingdoms and, although none of them remains to this day, quite a few of their sites have been located. As stated earlier, the nine-storied wooden pagoda on the site of Hwangnyong Temple in Kyŏngju was the tallest and the story of how this pagoda came to be constructed and how it stood until it was completely burnt to the ground early in the 13th century has been related in this article. Stone pagodas were first built in Paekche and then in Silla in different styles peculiar to each kingdom, but these styles all concern the outward appearances of the pagodas.

It must be stressed that these pagodas are the products of religious faith. Because pagodas contained the holy relics of Buddha, Buddhists naturally worshiped such pagodas. In fact, all pagodas still extant in Korea are said to have been erected as objects of worship, particularly so during the Three Kingdoms period. Because pagodas were built on the basis of religious faith and protected by the state as objects of worship, Korean pagodas, even after the temples they were originally part of were destroyed or burnt to the ground, were not removed from their original sites nor were they desecrated in anyway. The still-pervading taboo among the people that calamities will befall those who use pagodas for purposes other than religious worship or who dare to remove a pagoda from its original site, has resulted in pagodas built during the Three Kimgdoms period, more than one thousand years ago, still standing on their original sites. However, it is regrettable that not many of these pagodas are seen around the country in spite of the fact that ancient literature described Korea as "flights of wild geese."

Buddhist Thought and Architectural Design of Temples

AN KYE-HYŎN

Buddhist Temples of Koguryŏ

Buddhism was introduced from China into Korea in 372. Three years later two Buddhist temples were built; they were Ibullan-sa and Sŏngmun-sa temples which are considered to be the first in Korea.

In 393 nine national temples were built in the capital city and in 497, about one hundred years later, the great temple of Kŭmgang-sa was built. Besides these famous temples it is likely that in the capital city, as well as all over the country, temples were quite numerous. The ruins of the temple which was located in Ch'ŏng'am-ri in the Taedong river valley gives us an idea of the magnificence of this period's temples.

The excavations of 1938 and 1939 in Ch'ŏng'am-ri permitted us to learn the architectural design and the arrangement of the different buildings. Thus we know that on the southern side inside the surrounding fence there was a big eight-angled pagoda around which buildings were erected, and that they were linked to the pagoda by a narrow stone-paved path. On the north side of the pagoda three buildings were built side by side and it seems that the biggest one was erected in the center.

The arrangement of the various buildings inside the surrounding fence interests us in two ways: first of all, it is influenced by the astrological philosophy of China. Since the Han Empire's traditional astronomy not only expressed a vision of the universe but also had a religious meaning, its philosophical system based on the idea that there exists a close relationship between human life and astrological phenomena constitutes the basis of the spiritual life. The Five Stars Philosophy (五星思想) is a good illustration of this system. In the history book called *sagi* (史記) written by Szŭ Ma Ch'ien (司馬遷) the position of these five stars is well illustrated. The architectural design of the Ch'ŏng'am-ri Temple is drawn after this five-star pattern. The pagoda and the main sanctuary which were located in the north are connected by a paved way. They occupy the places named Hwangdo and Pukkung in the five-star pattern. We will be struck too by another fact: it is the ratio of the areas of the pagoda to the main temple. In the Ch'ŏng'am-ri Temple this area ratio is 0.7, whereas in the Sach'ŏn-wang Temple, built during the Silla kingdom, the area ratio is 0.4.

The pagoda is the place where remains (relics: sari) are preserved; the main shrine is the place where religious ceremonies are held. The fact that the Ch'ŏng'am-ri Temple's pagoda is larger than the one of the Sach'ŏn-wang Temple

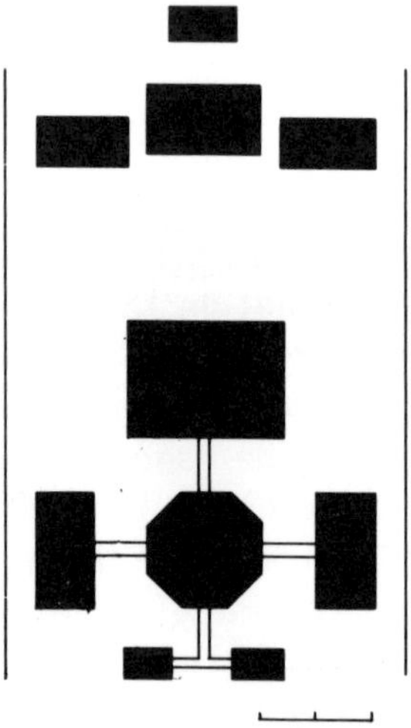

Disposition of a temple at Ch'ŏng'am-ri

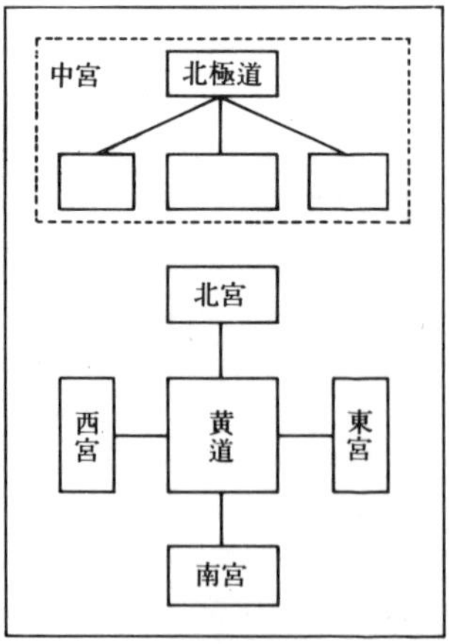

Scheme of the Five Stars Philosophy

would mean that the people of the Koguryŏ kingdom gave much more importance than their descendants to the preservation of remains (relics). In other words, we could say that the Koguryŏ kingdom people were more interested in the way the Buddha had spent his life and in the way he had became the Buddha than in the way the Buddha had taught, and what he taught about the way humans could be saved.

Paekche Buddhist Architectural Design

It was in 384 that Buddhism was introduced into the Paekche kingdom. For a century, until the moment when the Paekche kingdom's capital city was transferred to Kongju in 475 because of unceasing military attacks from Koguryŏ, it seems that a great number of temples would have been built along the Han River, though there remains no trace of them. To consolidate the kingdom, Paekche's capital city was once more transferred to Puyŏ in 538 after only 60 years in Kongju.

The ruins of the Taet'ong-sa Temple are famous but as they are nowadays incorporated in the modern city it is impossible to make excavations. However the temples of the Puyŏ period (538-660) have been much studied and the ruins of the temples show that all of them had pagodas. The buildings are arranged in a linear way from the south to the north as follows: the intermediate gate, the pagoda, the old temple (Kŭmdang) and the conference hall. The gold temple is another name for the Buddha's shrine (pŏbtang). Two wings of the intermediate gate are extended up to the conference hall; this gallery is a barrier against the outside world. The ruins of Kunsu-ri and of Tongnam-ri such as the temples of Chŏngrim-sa, Kŭmgang-sa and the ruins of Mirŭk-sa Temple were built after the same architectural pattern, though we can find a few exceptions such as the ruins of Kunsu-ri, in which a few buildings were built outside the surrounding gallery on the west and the east side of the Kŭmdang hall. We can notice too that the temple of

Tongnam-ri has no pagoda.

The architectural principles of the Paekche kingdom had a deep and lasting influence on the building of temples in ancient Japan.

The ruins of the temples of the Paekche kingdom have been thoroughly excavated. The excavations began at the ruins of Kunsu-ri. According to the results of studies made in 1935, it has been found that the architectural principle in the Kunsu-ri Temple was roughly similar to the one used in the Koguryŏ kingdom's Ch'ŏng'am-ri temple, though there are a few differences. Thus the intermediate gate, the pagoda, the main shrine, and the two buildings which are located outside of the surrounding gallery take the place of the stars in the five stars of the Chinese philosophical system. In the Korean temples they are called Namgung, Hwangdo, Pukkung, Tonggung and Sŏgung, so we can presume that the conference hall is a simplified reproduction of Chunggung. We can consider Kunsu-ri Temple as a kind of transition from Koguryŏ's

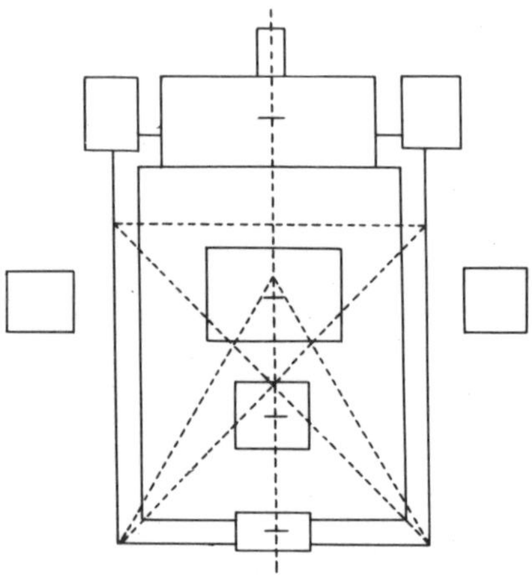

Disposition of a temple at Kunsu-ri

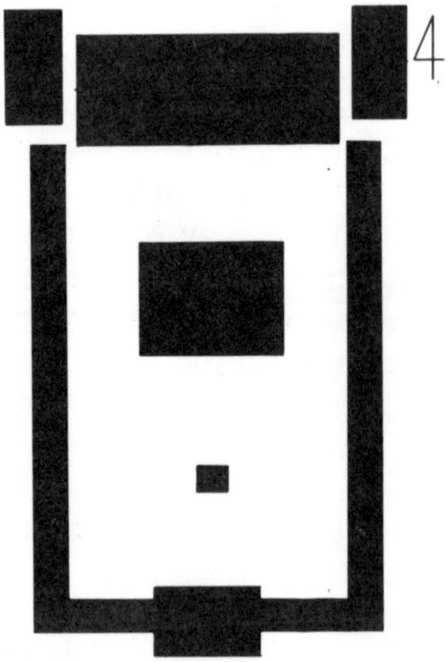

Plan of Chŏngrim-sa Temple

architectural principle towards the Paekche style which is trying to find its own way. In the Kunsu-ri Temple we can notice that the pagoda was placed in the center of an isosceles triangle whose basis was the southern gallery. This pagoda was located exactly in the middle of the median line drawn from the summit down to the basis of this isosceles triangle. Or we could also consider that the central part of the front of the pagoda which faced the Kŭmdang hall was located on the intersection point of the diagonal lines of a square whose sides were the surrounding galleries. It was in that way that the location and the dimensions of the pagoda were fixed. The distance between the intermediate gate and the pagoda is 18 meters, and the distance between the Kŭmdang hall and the pagoda is nine meters. The distance from the center of the intermediate gate to the center of the pagoda is exactly the same as the distance from the center of the pagoda to the center of the Kŭmdang hall or 24 meters. The distance from the center of the Kŭmdang hall to the center of the conference hall is 36 meters (24 × 1.5).

A. Chŏngrim-sa Temple in Puyŏ

Chŏngrim-sa too is built after the same principles and it has a pagoda, though, contrary to Kunsu-ri Temple, there is no building outside the surrounding gallery on the east or on the west. We could say that Chŏngrim-sa is a typical temple of the Paekche kingdom.

B. Kŭmgang-sa Temple in Puyŏ

This was also built according to the architectural principles adopted by the Paekche kingdom. However, it is exceptional in the fact that its front entrance faces toward the east, despite the fact that Paekche temples generally face the south, and that the buildings are disposed on a south-north line.

Kŭmgang-sa Temple's buildings are arranged on an east-west oriented line. The distance between the center of the intermediate gate and the center of the pagoda, on one hand, and the distance between the center of the pagoda and the center of the main shrine, on the other hand, is the same: 24 meters. But the distance from the center of the main shrine to the center of the conference hall is 48 meters (24 m × 2). This too is a peculiarity which makes Kŭmgang-sa Temple different from the other temples of its period.

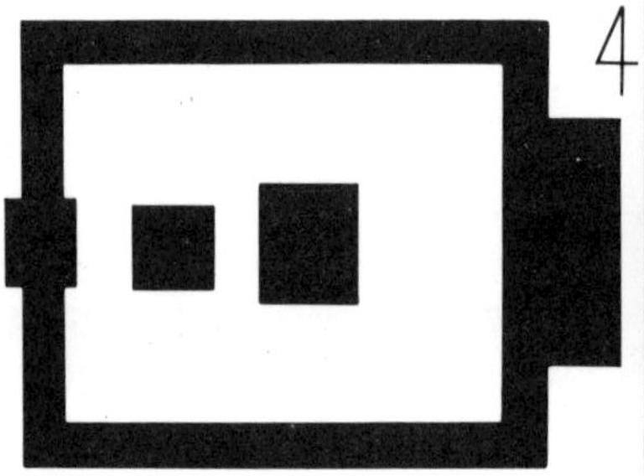

Disposition of Kŭmgang-sa Temple

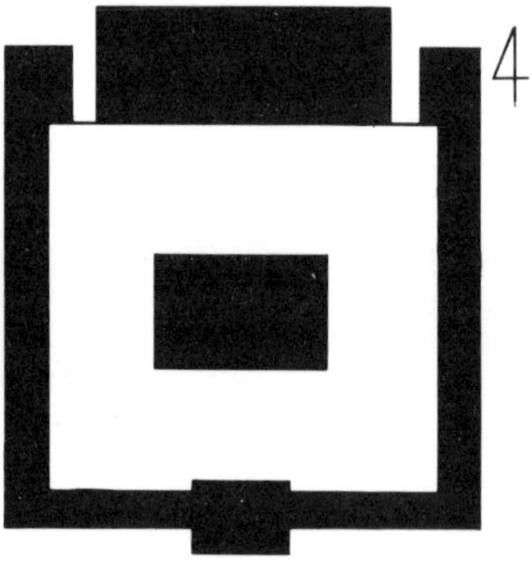

Plan of a temple at Tongnam-ri

C. Tongnam-ri Temple in Puyŏ

Though generally temples had a pagoda, in the ruins of Tongnam-ri Temple there is no trace of one. It is exceptional among Paekche temples.

The surrounding galleries which start from the sides of the intermediate gate go up to the two sides of the conference hall. The eastern, western and southern sides of the main shrine are all at the same distance from the surrounding gallery. Why is there no pagoda? For lack of sufficient evidence we cannot answer this question. But in the Silla kingdom temples too we can find such an example: it is Pusŏk-sa Temple, which has no pagoda because of the Avatamsaka thought and Amitabha faith. But we cannot assert that in the case of Tongnam-ri it is for the same reasons that no pagoda was built.

D. Ruins of Mirŭk-sa Temple in Iksan

Mirŭk Temple was the largest in Korea. On the south-north oriented line we could find the intermediate gate, the pagoda, the main shrine and the conference hall. The whole is surrounded by a gallery built after the Paekche architectural principles. But there are two more buildings, one on the west, the other on the east. Both are of the same size; on the northern side, too, there is a still bigger building. These three buildings were surrounded by walls.

Thus, Mirŭk Temple is made up of three parts which are named Tongt'abwŏn, Sŏt'abwŏn and Chungt'abwŏn. The most ancient pagoda in Korea is Sŏt'abwŏn.

Silla Temple Architecture

It was in 527 that the Silla kingdom officially adopted the Buddhist faith. Though this was somewhat later than Koguryŏ and Paekche, the Buddhist faith strongly influenced the kingdom's politics. People made of Buddhism the basis of their spiritual life. This is why Buddhism flourished here much more than in the two other kingdoms so far dealt with. The building of temples well illustrates this. After having defeated and conquered Paekche and Koguryŏ, Silla reunified the Korean peninsula and undertook the construction of many temples in the middle of the seventh century. The architecture of the temple is not different from that of Paekche. They were built after the same principles: on a south-north oriented line beginning with the intermediate gate, then the pagoda, the main shrine and at the end the conference hall. A gallery surrounded the whole.

Before the unification of the peninsula, these Silla temples had a single pagoda in front of the main shrine. But after unification, the pagodas were built side by side in front of the main shrine.

The Punhwang-sa and Hwangryong-sa temples in Kyŏngju, which were built before the Silla kingdom reached the peak of its prosperity, had a single pagoda. As to the gallery, at this time it linked the intermediate gate to the conference hall, though later the east and west galleries were linked too on both sides to the main building, so that the temple was divided into two parts: the northern part and the southern part. The distance between the buildings was determined by a well-defined rule. These are the characteristics of the temples built during the prosperity of Silla.

Why do these temples have two pagodas, one in the east and one in the west? One explanation would be that two pagodas instead of one help to make the design of the whole temples more balanced and harmonious. But it is not a very convincing explanation and we will have to look for another one. The two pagodas of Pulguk-sa Temple in Kyŏngju may give us a clue. During the height of Silla golden age the temples had two similarly shaped pagodas though we can see that the two pagodas of Pulguk-sa Temple are dissimilar in shape: the one on the east shows a greater originality. The pagoda situated on the east has been called Tabot'ab, (Pagoda of Prabhutaratna) and the one situated on the west has been called Sŏkkat'ab. The latter is built in testimony to the teachings of Sakyamuni Buddha, whereas the Tabot'ab is built in testimony to the truth that Sakyamuni has transmitted in his teachings.

Here we must clearly understand a few points of the teachings of the *Saddharma-pundarika Sutra*. In the first chapter it is said:

"While Sakyamuni was teaching, a big tower made out of seven treasures came out of the earth. The people who were standing there listening to the teachings were greatly surprised. Then from inside the tower a voice said that the teachings of Sakyamuni were the only truth. Then when

Sakyamuni opened the door of the pagoda he saw Prabhutaratna who was seated inside it. The latter, saying that he came to listen to the teachings, invited him to sit at his side. When he sat at his side the people standing there prayed to these two Buddhas.

In the second chapter of this same *Saddharma-pundarika Sutra* there are the following teachings: Truth is one, but the ability to understand being different from one individual to the other, Buddha gives people the choice between three different methods to understand the One Truth. Thus, though "the three" are temporarily used, "the one" is the only truth. Following these teachings of the *Saddharma-pundarika Sutra*, Silla may well have thought that it was necessary to destroy the two other kingdoms of Paekche and Koguryŏ to unify the peninsula into a great kingdom. Thus a close relationship exists between the Silla kingdom and the *Saddharma-pundarika Sutra*. This may explain why during the height of Silla's prosperity people showed deep devotion to *Saddharma-pundarika Sutra*. This ardent faith is well reflected in the architecture of the temples, which always had two pagodas. It is thought that in the Pulguk-sa Temple the two pagodas are dissimilarly shaped to draw the attention of onlookers.

A. *The Ruins of Ch'ŏn'gun-ri Temple*

About ten kilometers from Kyŏngju are located the ruins of a temple built during the golden age of Silla. In this temple the basic distance between the different buildings is 15 meters. Thus the distance from the south to the north is 75 meters (15m × 5). The distance from the east to the west is 60 meters (15m × 4). In the isosceles triangle whose basis is the south gallery, the summit is located in the center of the back wall of the main shrine, and the front wall of the main shrine is exactly thirty meters from the southern gallery.

B. The Ruins of Mangdŏk-sa Temple

The ruins of this temple are located in the neighborhood of Kyŏngju. In this temple the basic distance between the buildings is 17 meters. The gallery surrounds a square 68 meters on all sides (17 m × 4).

The two pagodas are erected on the spot where the north-south oriented lines which are drawn 17 meters from the eastern and western gallery intersect the east-west oriented line which is drawn 17 meters from the southern gallery. The area of the pagoda is 8.5 square meters.

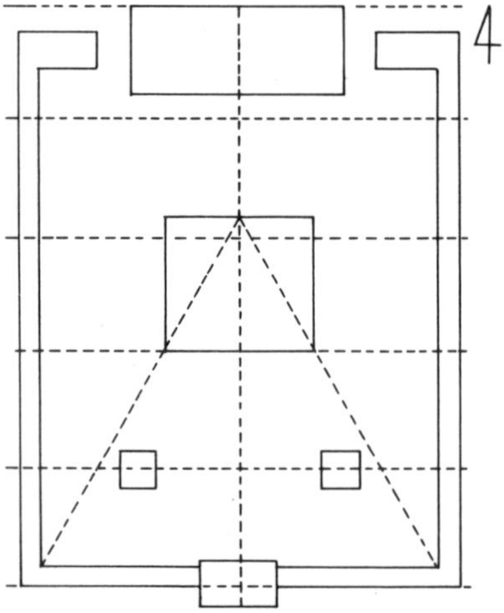

Disposition of a temple at Ch'ŏn'gun-ri

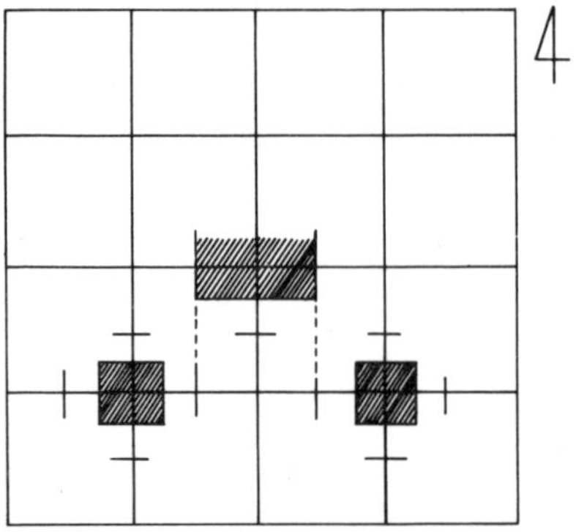

Disposition of Mangdŏk-sa Temple

C. The Ruins of Kamŭn Temple

These are located not far from Kyŏngju on the eastern side of the city. This temple has two typical pagodas from the period of the beginning of Silla's golden age. This temple is characterized by the fact that its north-south length is less than its east-west width. This would come from topographical conditions.

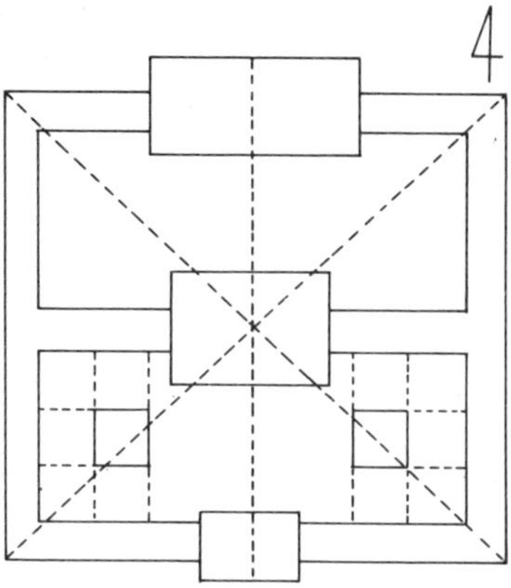

Plan of Kamŭn-sa Temple

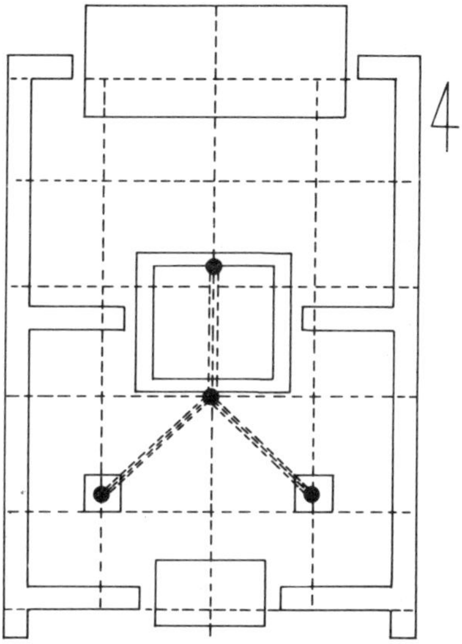

Plan of Pulguk-sa Temple

The main shrine was linked to the surrounding galleries by two side galleries, and the center of the main shrine happens to be the center of the whole temple. The sides of the pagodas are all situated at exactly the same distance from the surrounding galleries' sides.

D. Pulguk-sa Temple in Kyóngju

Pulguk-sa is located at the foot of T'oham mountain and is the only existing temple which can show us the architecture of the golden age of the Silla kingdom.

In Pulguk-sa the basic measure is 13 meters. The north-south length is 65 meters (13m × 5). The east-west width is 52 meters (13m × 4). In this temple there is a central gallery which links the lateral galleries to the main shrine. The bottom of the stairs which go up to the main shrine is located 26 meters from the southern gallery.

This point of intersection is at an equal distance from the

back side of the main shrine and from each of the pagodas. The southern side of the pagodas is 13 meters from the southern gallery. Pulguk-sa Temple also has buildings located outside the gallery. On the north side of the northern gallery Kwanŭm-jŏn and Piro-jŏn are to be found. Outside of the southern gallery Kŭngnak-chŏn is located. In the Piro-jŏn Vairocana is placed and in Kwanŭm-jŏn Avalokiteishvara. Vairocana is the Buddha symbolizing the philosophy of the *Avatamsaka Sutra*. On the other hand, the teachings of the Avalokiteishvara are in *Saddharma-pundarika Sutra*. According to the 25th chapter of the latter, if we believe in Avalokiteishvara we shall not only be protected from damages caused by fire and water, but also we shall be granted all the things we wish.

What draws attention is Kŭngnak-chŏn where Amitabha resides. The staircase going down from the western gallery is made up of three sets of 16 steps. According to the *Sukhavativiyuha Sutra*, the Land of Purity, or Paradise (Sukhavati), is situated far in the west where Amitabha governs. If we want to go there after death we must fulfill sixteen obligations. But as abilities are different from one individual to the other, they have been divided into three types. This is why Kŭngnak-chŏn is built to the west of Pulguk-sa Temple, and the stairs which go up from the main shrine to the paradise shrine (Kŭngnak-chŏn) are made up of three sets of 16 steps. This architectural design well reflects the teachings of the Sutras.

Pulguk-sa is the only temple of the Silla golden age which has been preserved in its original aspect. It can be considered as a synthesis of Buddhist philosophies. These are the reasons which give to this temple such a tremendous importance.

The Architecture of the Koryŏ Temples

The Silla kingdom was followed by the Koryŏ kingdom

(916-1392) which protected Buddhism and thus during this period many famous temples were built. During the first half of the dynasty the architecture followed the architectural principles of Silla.

The buildings were arranged according to a south-north oriented line on which we find the intermediate gate, the main shrine and the conference hall. The gallery which linked the conference hall to the intermediate gate defined the exterior boundary of the temple. But in the second half of the dynasty this basic principle was modified and the buildings were erected without any definite architectural principles, being arranged according to the possibilities offered by the local topographical conditions. The gallery disappeared in most newly-built temples. Hŭngwang-sa Temple, built in 1067 at Kaesŏng, well symbolizes the architecture of the first half of the dynasty. Except in Paekche's Kŭmgang Temple, since the Koguryŏ dynasty the pagoda had traditionally been built on the south of the main shrine. We have seen that the temples of the Silla period had two pagodas on the south of the main shrine. This tradition had been followed in the case of Hŭngwang-sa, which has two pagodas too, though in the Pulil-sa Temple built in 951 there is only one pagoda. But what is to be noticed is the fact that this pagoda is not located on the southern side of the main shrine, but on an east-west line on the side of the main shrine. The ruins of Yŏnbuk-sa at Kaesŏng and of Manbok-sa at Namwŏn are examples which well illustrate this fact. The former has its pagoda located on the western side of the main building and the latter on the eastern side. It would seem that this kind of arrangement was intended to give the same importance to the main building and to the pagoda. On the other hand Hoeam-sa, built in 1376, is a typical example of the second half of the Koryŏ dynasty. This is a quite original temple in that it does not at all follow the traditional architectural principle of other Buddhist temples. The intermediate gate, the main shrine and the conference hall are all located on a south-north oriented line. The shrine where the remains (relics) are kept takes the place of the pagoda and is located on the north of the conference hall. This shrine where the relics are kept is a building made of wood which has the same role as the pagodas made of stone.

On the northern side of this building Nahan-jŏn is built. Arhat is placed in this construction. Arhat is used as another name for the Buddha in the "great vehicle" (Mahayana) doctrine, whereas in the "small vehicle" (Hinayana) doctrine it means a righteous man who has understood the truth but who is not the Buddha. Besides this, in the Hoeam-sa Temple there are Chosa-jŏn built on the side of the conference hall and in front of the intermediate gate; Mit'a-jŏn, and Kwanŭm-jŏn built respectively on the east and west side. Chosa-jŏn is a shrine especially built to the memory of a few famous monks of this temple. Their pictures are hung on the wall.

Modern Buddhist Temples

Most of the temples we can see nowadays on the Korean peninsula were built or rebuilt during the Yi dynasty or even afterwards. When rebuilding the temples the traditional principle of the arrangement of the buildings has been sacrificed to make the temple well adapted to the topographical conditions and to the specific function of the buildings. If we try to find out a common feature among these rebuilt temples and the ancient ones we might point out that the main shrine called Taeung-jŏn, which is the place where the Buddha is seated and which corresponds to the pŏbtang of ancient temples, is to be found at the far end inside the surrounding walls. In front of the garden of Taeung-jŏn on the right and the left there are monks' cells, and the intermediate gate is on the backside of a pagoda which is in front of Taeung-jŏn.

Throughout, what is of interest to us are not these common

features regarding the arrangement of the buildings, but the fact which should be pointed out is that in most temples, inside the intermediate gate there are sculptures of Sach'ŏn-wang. And often we can also find Myŏngbu-jŏn, Ch'ilsŏng-gak and Sansin-gak which are in the corners. Sach'ŏn-wang are the generals who keep guard on the four cardinal points. The west is kept by Chiguk-ch'ŏnwang, (Dhritarastra) the south by Chunggangch'ŏn. (Virudhaka). These two guards hold swords in their right hands. The one who keeps guard to the west is named Kwangmok-ch'ŏnwang (Virupaksha); he holds a writing brush and a scroll of paper in each hand. The one who keeps the north is Tamun-ch'ŏnwang (Vaishravana); he holds a spear and a tower in each hand. These four generals take a terrifying attitude and under their feet small demons are crushed to death. It is obvious, they are there inside the intermediate gate to protect the temple. On the other hand in Myŏngbu-jŏn are placed the ten kings and Chijang-bosal (Ksitigarbha).

Buddhism teaches that at the resurrection time we will go to paradise if we have been virtuous during our life, but if we have not been virtuous during our earthly life we will go to Hell (Naraka) and we will never get out of there again. Yŏmnadaewang (Yamaraja) and the ten kings are the judges. Chijang-bosal who stands there too holds out a saving hand to the sinners sentenced to Hell; it is why Chijang-bosal was very popular, mostly among the people who had no deep knowledge about Buddhism. He was the savior who saved them from going to hell.

During the Yi dynasty as Buddhism was oppressed his popularity decreased. Because of the popular belief in Chijang-bosal, Buddhism has a strong and lasting influence on the people's life. This popular belief is also a means for men to get rid of the terror of solitude and uneasiness with which fatality oppressed him.

Besides these four generals, the ten kings and Chijang-bosal, there are Ch'ilsŏng-gak and Sansin-gak. The former is erected in praise to the seven stars of the Big Dipper and the latter to the Mountain God. Since the Koryŏ dynasty these stars have been prayed to for long life and happiness. The Mountain God had been believed in since very ancient times. These beliefs, linked to Buddhism, made their entrance inside the temples. The belief in Chijang-bosal, the Big Dipper, and the Mountain God played an important role to consolidate Buddhism among the popular masses during the Yi dynasty when Buddhism was repressed. Nowadays too we can see that there is still a strong link between Buddhism and these popular beliefs.

2,000-Year History of Korean Ceramics

CH'OE SUN-U

In the history of Korean handicrafts ceramics take pride of place, not merely because archaeologists have found more examples of these than of other types of handicraft but also because it would appear that from the beginning (the fourth or fifth century) considerable emphasis was placed on aesthetic principles in the construction and design of baked clay artefacts.

Korean ceramics has a 2,000 year history, ranging from the Three Kingdoms period (Koguryŏ, Paekche, Silla) through the flowering of celadon in the Koryŏ period and the great advances in porcelain (Punch'ŏng and white porcelains) which characterized the Yi period. Although at all times influenced by the Chinese developments, especially the southern ceramic traditions, Korean ceramics maintained a naturalness of colour, a sense of freedom and unaffected simplicity which remains today its outstanding merit.

Earthenware in the Three Kingdoms Period

Our knowledge of Koguryŏ earthenware comes from a small number of remains excavated from fifth and sixth century tombs such as that on Mount Mandal in Taedong, South P'yŏngan Province. These remains consist of mostly pot-like vessels intended for practical use. Their construction represents the style of China's later Han bronze vessels, and they were made on a spinning wheel. They are grayish black or grayish brown soft earthenware and were baked at a low temperature. In terms of design some vessels showed a simple wave pattern and the surfaces were polished and there are some examples of glazed ware.

Many more examples of Paekche pottery have been excavated and these reflect more varied skills in baking, some at high temperatures, some soft ware baked at low temperatures and examples of glazed vessels. Some sophistication in construction is evidenced by the variety of shapes; some of the vessels are lidded, they often have three legs which are ornamented with animal faces and a mountainscape after the Six Dynasties pattern. These are also round clay inkstones supported by animal-like legs. In the latter part of the period functional flat-bottomed pots and trays are more common.

From the latter part of the sixth century Paekche earthenware reflected the styles of Sui and T'ang ware. They have stamped checkered patterns and straw mat designs strewn with horizontal lines. The clay used in Paekche earthenware was more refined that the Silla or Koguryŏ clay and the spinning wheel techniques evidence considerable maturity. The potters had developed the art of refining the clay through water and using reduction firing. Glazed (a soft lead glaze introduced from the north) earthenware, baked at both high and low temperatures, is also to be found.

The Old Silla earthenware, having developed from the preceding Kimhae tradition, evolved its own unique style by the latter half of the fourth century. These vessels are still excavated in large numbers and are divided into two groups, those from the east and those from the west of the Naktong River. One type are clay vessels baked in a reducing flame, the other are greyish black pottery. The water sifting process was not yet perfected so the Silla wares were somewhat porous coarse. Silla patterns were most commonly geometric, lined, or waved with some dot patterns carved in sharp intaglio. In exceptional cases there are some rudimentary human and animal figures. The shapes also varied on either side of the river, long necked pots with round bottoms or stands to the east and pots without stands to the west, orifices for ventilation round or oblong in the east, triangular in the west. It is assumed that smaller vessels in the shape of humans, animals, boats etc. were intended for ceremonial use. The style of the Silla artifacts reflect more ancient Northeast Asian styles and also the style of the Warring Period of China.

Earthenware in the Unified Silla Period

The earthenware of the Unified Silla became much more functional and practical, round-bottomed and long-necked ports, high-legged goblets and ceremonial ware, made room for pots, vases, round bowls and cups. Stamped floral patterns, later a conspicuous feature of the Unified Silla ware, began to replace the patterns of lines in sharp intaglio. Retaining the influence of the Six Dynasties and T'ang ceramics they showed conspicuous changes in styles and patterns. One characteristic change was that bowls are all shallow in depth and broad in diameter in the stand part and voluminous in overall appearance with fat hemispherical lids in most cases. The stamped floral patterns include strawrope screen, necklace, willow leaves (from Persian art via China), flower petal dot and gem patterns.

Tiles and Bricks (Three Kingdoms-Unified Silla)

The development of wooden architecture resulted in a rising demand for tiles and bricks for roofs and interior decoration.

In Koguryŏ tiles, lotus flower, grass, animal faces and

honeysuckle patterns are common and they are carved with deep, simple and forceful strokes. The influence is that of the Chinese Lolang tile and, later, the Wei style where the tile is divided into four or six equal parts, decorated with one lotus flower carved in sharp relief.

Paekche tiles strongly show the influence of the Six Dynasties' single petal lotus pattern, while occasional examples of Koguryŏ-type petal patterns or the Buddhist swastika are to be found. Perhaps it was in brick-making that Paekche made the most significant advances. The eight square ornamental painted bricks discovered in 1973, in Oe-ri, Kyuam-myŏn, Puyŏ are a good example from the first half of the seventh century. Patterns, (lotus, clouds, dragons, two kinds of demons, two kinds of landscapes), are carved in relief and show a high degree of skill. Bricks carved with honeysuckle, geometric and lotus patterns belong to the same group as those founded from the Southern Chinese Liang dynasty.

The development of palaces and temples in the Unified Silla period induced a greater diversification of design and maturity of technique in both tile and brick. The single lotus petal moved from pairs of petals to the whole flower with leaves, and move sophisticated and imaginative carving of animals, humans, animals in landscape settings began to emerge. A characteristic of this period is the development in tile and brick, of the carving of the faces of demons to mature three-dimensional expression. The developments in brick making followed apace, for example the arabesque pattern excavated in Imhae-jŏn Hall, Kyŏngju, or the image of the four Deva kings in green, glazed brick discovered in the ruin of Sach'ŏnwang-sa Temple, also in Kyŏng-ju. The carvings of the United Silla period are evidence of the influence of T'ang sculpture.

Koryŏ Ceramics

The remains of a kiln for making glazed grey earthenware dating from the Unified Silla period was discovered in Kyŏngju in 1974. The existence of this glazed earthenware and the techniques of producing it made it easier for Koryŏ to absorb the Chinese art of making blue celadons.

The Chinese techniques came from two areas early in the tenth century. The northern Chinese technique moved from Shantung province across the Yellow Sea to Inch'ŏn, Kyŏnggi Province, Sŏsan in South Ch'ungch'ŏng Province and Hwanghae Province along the west coast. This type of earthenware from this influence is called green blue celadon for the glaze used is coarse and dark green and when baked the glaze is congealed here and there on the surface of the ware making it coarse. The clay used was light and grey soil, and they were baked by reduction firing. The shapes followed the late T'ang style.

The other influence was the Yuehchou technique from the Hangchou Bay area and it moved to the southwest coast of Korea to Puan, North Chŏlla province and Kangjin, South Chŏlla province and moved inland. The earthenware produced by this technique was blue celadon baked by reduction firing.

Below we will examine briefly the development of Koryŏ ceramics.

From the early 10th to the late 11th century

During the tenth century Korean celadons were still very immature. The attempt was made to produce white porcelains in imitation of T'ang ware glazed in grey and glazed with lead along with some grey-blue wave. Remains of these have been excavated from tombs such as Tomb no. 2 in Ch'ŏnbu-dong on Ullŭng Island. Extant examples are a small, glazed blue sarira container dating from 983 A.D. and another sarira container dating from 1031 A.D. discovered in a stone pagoda in Chongdu Temple. A celadon pot dating from the fourth year of the Sunhwa Era is considered illustrative of the formative period of Koryŏ celadon production. It is in fact more akin to a white porcelain than to a celadon in view of the quality of its clay.

Chapters on Koryŏ in the *History of Sung* would also indicate that while porcelain was being made the everyday vessels and dishes of this period were made of copper. Another report by Fujio Koyama says that fragments of a Koryŏ celadon dating from C. 1031 were found in a king's tomb in Manchuria indicating that by this time the production of porcelain was more established and of sufficient quality to be sought by the royal family of a foreign kingdom.

The later 11th to the later 12th century

It was in this period that Koryŏ's unique pure blue glaze known as jade color was properly refined. The kingdom of Koryŏ, in the period after 1083, had close cultural ties with North Sung whose ceramics were very highly developed, a fact which greatly stimulated the refinement of Koryŏ celadons. According to a report in the *History of Sung* dating from 1113, the demand for celadon became so great that many hard-pressed potters abandoned their profession. Another report in the *Koryŏ Tuching* (c. 1123) describes the celadon in detail and examples of this ware were discovered in the tomb of King Injong who died in 1140. This ware is pure celadon without inlaid design. Although there are some patterns carved in relief or in intaglio, they are simple.

The best work was produced from the kilns of Kangjin and Puan. As well as the jade celadon greenish white porcelains, celadons with carved paintings, celadons with tree branch pattern and celadons with underglaze iron were produced. Also in the 12th century the influence of northern Chinese ware such as that produced in Tingchou, Juchou, Lungchuan, and Yochou began to influence the shape of Koryŏ celadons. Inlaying techniques, painted pottery and the technique of underglaze iron and oxidized copper, which involved painting on the bare clay and then coating it with blue glaze, were developed. The technique of inlaying was original to Koryŏ celadons.

The later 12th to the later 13th century

The latter half of the 12th century witnessed the zenith of prosperity of inlaid celadon which was produced by the following process; the pattern was carved in intaglio on the clay base and the engraved lines were filled in with red clay pigment (which includes oxidized iron) and white clay pigment which were then coated with a blue glaze. The vessels were then baked, the red clay turning into black and the white clay into white.

Examples of this inlaid celadon were excavated from the tomb of King Myŏngjong who died in 1187.

The characteristic of the period up to the Mongol invasion of 1231 was the wide variety in pottery production from pure celadon, to inlaid celadon, white porcelains, celadons decorated with underglazed gold and (from the middle of the 13th century) celadons with underglazed copper, and iron glazed ware of a reddish brown colour as well as the glazed black ware which came on from the Silla period. This black glaze was unique to Korea.

In the latter half of the 13th century, with the kingdom of Koryŏ under Mongol control, the production of pottery fell into decline, paralleling a similar decline in China. This decline continued throughout to the late 14th century.

Yi Dynasty Ceramics

The art of ceramics in the early part of the Yi dynasty was

characterized by the production of hard white porcelains and they were greatly influenced by the Ming Chinese technique of making white porcelains with underglaze blue. These Yi vessels, while being less elaborate than the Koryŏ ware, reflected a transformation from aristocratic taste to free, practical and functional styles. There are two distinct periods in Yi dynasty ceramics. They are divided by the Hideyoshi invasion.

The late 14th century to the late 16th century

The dominant social idea of the Yi period was Confucianism and this shift from the leisurely and aristocratic Koryŏ to the more pragmatic social concepts of Confucianism is reflected in the ceramic art of the period. The inlaid celadons were once again produced in the Punch'ŏng style and the Ming-influenced white porcelains were the dominant style of the Yi period. Sŏng Hyŏn observed in Yongjae Ch'onghwa that, "all vessels used at the royal court during the reign of King Sejong were white porcelains." The difficulty with white porcelain was obtaining the needed blue glaze. King Sejo imported it but he also ordered his potters to mine a domestic ore which was believed to produce this blue glaze. The kilns were government controlled, and they produced inlaid white porcelains as well as inlaid blue celadons. There are considerable differences between Koryŏ and Yi porcelain both in the types of pattern and in the shapes. Yi white porcelains in underglaze blue were decorated with the pattern of the four gracious plants (plum blossom, orchid, chrysanthemums and bamboo) and with the lotus flower, arabesque and autumn grass. In the 15th century Korea produced ceramic articles in huge quantities. King Sejong's annals in *Yissi Wangjo Sillok* contains the information that there were 136 central and provincial kilns for Punch'ŏng porcelains.

Punch'ŏng porcelains were made of clay which contained a larger amount of iron than the clay for celadons. The rough surface of the Punch'ŏng clay was brushed with white slip and then coated with the transparent glaze before being baked. The glaze on Punch'ŏng clay ware shows traces of oxidization and this is because the rule of using only reduction firing was not always observed and in many cases the ware was baked on neutralized flames. The decorative motifs of Punch'ŏng porcelains can be summarized as follows: 1) White slip was brushed so naturally that the marks of the brush can be appreciated; 2) Before baking the ware was soaked in white slip so that the soft effect of the white color can be appreciated; 3) Before the baked vessels were dried a seal with a pattern was pressed on all of the surface, or a knife was employed to engrave a designed pattern and the carved patterns were filled in with white slip in order to create the effect of inlaying; 4) Patterns were carved with a knife on the white slip pasted on a vessel and then the white slip between patterns was scraped off in order to make the pattern look more outstanding; and 5) After decoration with a brush, a picture or a pattern was painted on the surface with red slip.

The early 17th century to 1910

The latter part of the Yi dynasty saw the nation's ceramic production unable to recover from the paralysis caused by the seven-year Japanese invasion which began in 1592. The war annihilated Punch'ŏng ware which had been continuously produced for 200 years. Many Korean potters and their families were abducted to Japan where they gave birth to Japanese porcelain ware in Kyushu.

After the invasion earthenware were mainly porcelains with some black-glazed ware produced mainly in provincial kilns. The white porcelains comprised pure white porcelains and those in underglaze blue. However the difficulty of obtaining the blue glaze forced the potters to experiment with underglaze iron which was especially developed during the 17th century. There were also white porcelains in underglaze copper with themes based on lotus flowers, chrysanthemums and feathered animals.

In the closing years of the reign of King Sukchong (r. 1674-1720) Yi dynasty ceramic production took on new life and the government kiln at Kwangju was restored to its former activity, under the influence of the Ch'ing culture then in full bloom in China. Initially Korea had rejected Ch'ing influence but their later importation of it provided the stimulus for Korean potters to rejuvenate their art. This cultural renaissance bloomed through the reign of kings Yŏngjo and Chŏngjo, and the earthenware was white porcelain in underglaze blue produced mainly through the government kilns in Kwangju.

In and after the mid-19th century Korea's ceramic art deteriorated in both technique and shape paralleling the decline of the nation itself. The day finally came when the

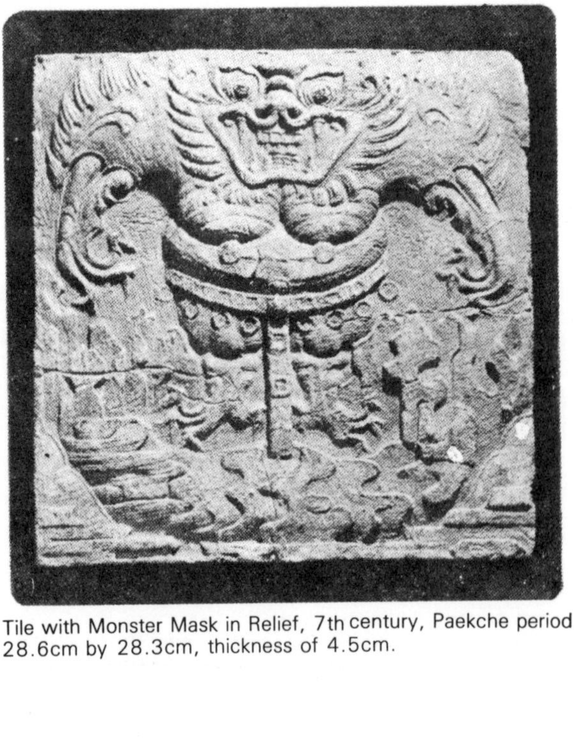

Tile with Monster Mask in Relief, 7th century, Paekche period. 28.6cm by 28.3cm, thickness of 4.5cm.

Kwangju kilns which had been playing a pivotal role were sold by the central government to a private company. Japanese potters were brought to Korea from Japan in an effort to modernize the Kwangju kilns, but the project ended in failure and the kilns were closed, after having been in existence for 500 years.

Pottery Arts of Unified Silla

CH'OE SUN-U

The Unified Silla period (668-935 A.D.) saw the emergence of artists and artisans whose eminence cannot be equalled throughout the remainder of the 2,000-year history of Korean fine arts. Their highly refined artistic motives and mature techniques of expression rank them among the best artists of the world, and in some fields Silla artists and artisans far excelled the handicraft techniques of their T'ang Chinese counterparts. Especially, Silla tiles and bricks are masterpieces of Oriental art. In terms of basic style tiles and bricks, like the pottery pieces of the period in general, embody the influences of T'ang art, but in their surface patterns they show more elaborate and diversified techniques than do Chinese pieces. Silla earthenware reached unique heights in terms of decoration.

The brilliant handicraft art of the Unified Silla period exerted a profound influence on Japan where the impact of Silla influence was felt more strongly than T'ang Chinese influence. Due to these interactions, the handicraft arts of the three countries consisted of a common basic style. Based on this common keynote, the three nations achieved unique development reflecting their respective national characteristics and the natural features of their lands.

Earthenware

With Silla's own social evolution and with the introduction

of T'ang culture, Silla earthenware gradually rid itself of the decorative and the illusory and developed into the functional and utilitarian styles of T'ang. Namely, beginning in the seventh century, the following metamorphosis took place in Silla earthenware:

First, the openings bored through the tall support of decorative Silla earthenware pieces became smaller and finally disappeared.

Second, the surface decorations on ancient earthenware, which consisted mainly of linear patterns, were replaced by circular, jewel, petal, leaf, straw rope, cloud, bird and animal patterns. The incised patterns of Silla are unique in that the

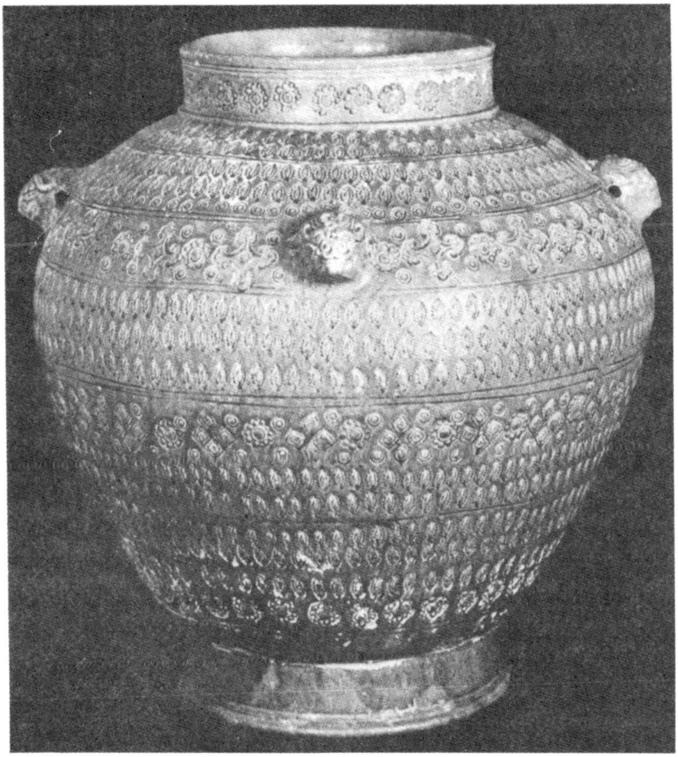

Burial urn, grey earthenware covered with an olive ash glaze. Height 39cm, diameter 37cm, 8th—9th century

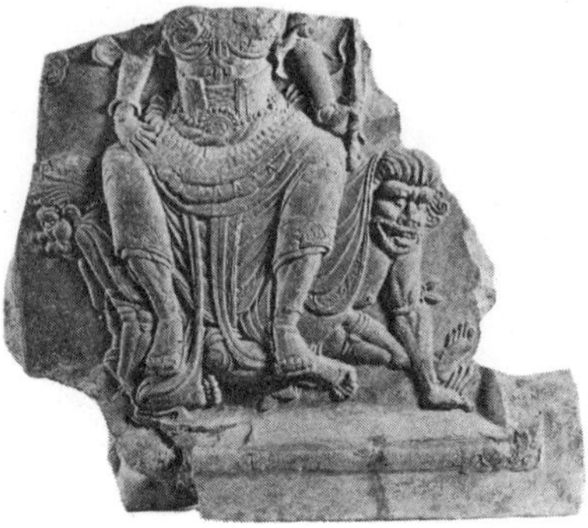

Sculptured tile, 7th century, height 53cm, width 60.7cm

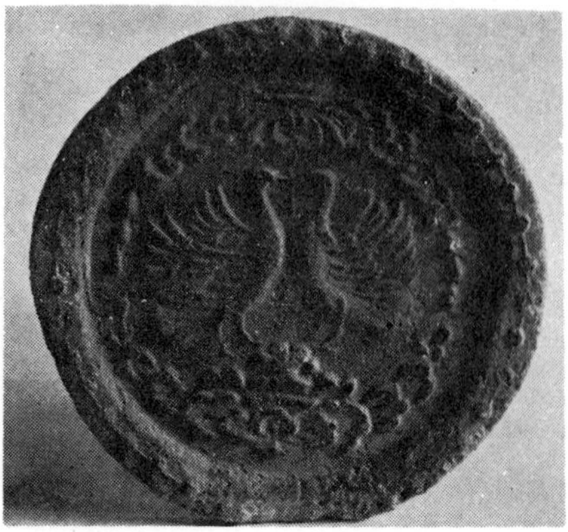

Twin bird patterned tile, 7th—8th century

same designs are placed in juxtaposition. Some patterns are painted in white to make them stand out.

Third, glazed earthenware was produced for the first time in this period. Most glazed ware is less solid as it was baked at low temperatures. Glazing was applied in many colors such as green and yellowish brown. It is presumed that Silla acquired her glazing techniques from Paekche where glazed earthenware of the T'ang style was produced before the downfall of that dynasty.

Fourth, most Silla earthenware now extant consists of urns. The demand for urns grew as cremation came into vogue from the middle of the seventh century. The urns are of many shapes—box, jar, long-necked bottle, pot with a tripod assuming the shape of the legs of a beast, a cylinder, and a high-stemmed goblet. Box- or jar-like urns have lids in the shape of a ball with the top suggesting flame, a pagoda or a little bottle, and most of them are glazed. In many cases, each lid has four tiny handles with holes placed in its four corners, through which cord was passed to seal the urn.

Fifth, many of the earthen boxes with semi-global lids, long-necked bottles, bowls, and pots with a tripod in the shape of the legs of a beast faithfully reflect the Sui and T'ang styles. This is indicative of the fact that Silla earthenware as an art was influenced by the styles of Sui and T'ang pottery and metal works and by the styles of Paekche earthenware as represented by the works of that dynasty's closing period.

Sixth, in most cases earthen urns are found on the slopes of mountains as they were buried inside a small stone casket in burial grounds. Funeral accessories made of clay, other than urns, were in most cases excavated from the stone chambers of larger tombs where corpses were buried. Most representative of such accessories are the earthenware pieces excavated from the stone chambers of the group of 10 ancient tombs in Ch'unghyo-ri, Kyŏngju, in 1932 by Japanese Professor Kyoichi Arimitsu. These Silla relics (refer to *A Report on Research on Ancient Stone Tombs in Ch'unghyo-ri, Kyŏngju*, by Kyoichi Arimitsu, Seoul, 1932) are, generally speaking, of the same style as urns in terms of decoration and basic form. They differ from urns only in size and design according to usage.

Seventh, as the art of celadon making, which was developed in China in ancient times, was introduced to Korea only in the 10th century, there are no celadon products dating back to the Silla period. However, among recently excavated relics in Korea there are, though very few, Chinese porcelain pieces dating back to the Six Dynasties period and Sui and T'ang.

Eighth, several of the tricolored T'ang pottery pieces which were in vogue in China at that time are preserved in *Shosoin*, the royal museum in Japan, together with some Japanese made imitations. However, no tricolored T'ang porcelain works have been found to date among Silla relics, and there are also no remains of kilns where imitation T'ang porcelain was made.

Ninth, while most Silla earthenware represents Unified Silla's own newly-developed style based on imported Chinese techniques, there is another group which maintains the ancient style of the Three Kingdoms period. This group includes an earthenware piece with a handle fixed to one side, an undecorated item, and one molded into shape with a wooden hammer.

Roof Tiles

The ever-expanding national strength of the newly emerged kingdom of Silla in the wake of completing the colossal task of unifying Korean peninsula, and its surging will to achieve cultural eminence gave rise to the construction of large Buddhist temples and pompous royal palaces in rapid succession. With this construction boom the demand for roofing and flooring tiles grew rapidly. Under such animated circumstances Silla artisans further refined and elevated the skills they had inherited from the Three Kingdoms period. Although they were greatly influenced by the architectural and handicraft techniques of the Sui and T'ang dynasties, they did not remain within the boundary of mere imitation but established their own unique and brilliant art of making tiles and gave tiles a prominent position in Unified Silla fine arts.

Roof tiles—The size and decorations of roof tiles differ according to the scale of an edifice or according to their usage. Unified Silla roof tiles are unsurpassed in their diversity and elaborateness and in the refinement of their patterns. The roof tiles of the T'ang dynasty which epitomized the golden era in the history of Chinese fine arts, as are the products of other periods of China, the birthplace of wooden architecture, are simple in terms of pattern. Japanese roof tiles produced in the corresponding period are decorated in the main by simple lotus flower patterns and cannot compete with Silla products in both quality and content.

As for the artistic value of Silla roof tiles some argue that the elaborateness, delicate patterns, and extraordinary refinement they embody are not necessary in view of the fact that they are placed out of normal view for close scrutiny. However, it is considered that the independent beauty each roof tile has is a product of Silla artisans' love of art and pride which made them ignore visual effect. This surprisingly beautiful artistic skill made Japanese artists of the Nara period long for Korean culture. It also goes without saying that Silla roof tiles demonstrated the artistic ability of the Korean people to Chinese envoys visiting the Silla kingdom.

Silla roof tiles are classified into the "male" tile (round), the "female" tile (flat), the demon-faced tile, and the falcon-head tile.

The spiritual content of roof tiles differs according to the buildings they graced. Namely, in the case of a Buddhist temple they embody veneration to Buddha and consist of motives to expel the vicious and uphold the auspicious. In the case of a royal palace, they depict the spirit to enhance the dignity of the monarch and symbolize his and his family's prosperity, as well as expelling the vicious and upholding the auspicious. The most common roof tile patterns are the lotus flower of male tiles and modifications of the same pattern. This indicates the Buddhist nature of the Silla kingdom.

Male roof tiles are divided into two groups according to patterns: the lotus-flower pattern and the animal pattern. They are also classified into circular and oval tiles.

Female tiles are classified into three groups: the arabesque-fairy pattern, the beast-fairy pattern, and the pattern of beast faces. We shall now explain in detail the development of each of these roof tiles and their classification:

(A) **The lotus-flower pattern** — This is the most common roof tile pattern of the Silla era. It is presumed that this pattern was developed and applied to roof tiles in China on the basis of Buddhist architectural designs introduced to China from India together with Buddhism. However, very few Chinese roof tiles bearing this ancient lotus-flower pattern remain today. Among these roof tiles the most outstanding are those excavated in Hsiushan Park in Nanking, in the Yünkang Stone Cave in Tatung, and in the tomb of Emperor Taitsung of T'ang. Retaining the most elegant ancient style are the Nanking tiles which are presumed to be products of the Six Dynasties period. The tiles excavated in the royal tomb show well-balanced proportion and a refinement worthy of T'ang masterpieces.

These Chinese roof tiles became the prototype of Silla products for they exerted a profound influence on Silla artisans. The Silla roof tiles to which the lotus-flower pattern was applied also inherit the traditions of Paekche tile making while being patterned after T'ang products. Deriving their inspiration from these two schools, the roof tiles made by Silla artisans finally reached the stage where they surpassed both the Chinese and the Paekchean products in terms of design and technique. The lotus-flower pattern is subdivided as follows:

- Single-petal pattern
  - Without marks
  - With marks
- Compound-petal pattern
- Double-petal pattern
  - Single leaf
    - Without marks
    - With marks
  - Compound leaf
- Combination of single and compound leaves

(B) **The arabesque pattern**—More often than not the arabesque pattern is found in flat tiles. This design is divided into the *Jentung* arabesque, the grape arabesque, the floral medallion arabesque and miscellaneous flower patterns. Flat tiles were decorated with these patterns toward the close of the Six Dynasties period or during the Sui and T'ang dynasties period. This decoration became the vogue in Unified Silla with the introduction of Chinese flat roof tiles.

Relics of the *Jentung* arabesque pattern were excavated in the Imhae-jŏn Pavilion and in the remains of Hwangnyong and Sach'ŏn-wang temples in Kyŏngju, all of them outstanding masterpieces. This pattern consists of elegant but natural lines and its design manifests a realistic and highly mature technique.

The grape arabesque pattern, originating in Southwest Asia, was developed in China and gained popularity in Korea during the Unified Silla period. Most eminent among relics belonging to this type are those excavated in the temple at Inwang-ni, Kyŏngju, and the ruins of Sach'ŏn-wang Temple. A cluster of grapes and grape vines alternate or there are stalks alone in this design.

The floral medallion arabesque pattern emerged in the wake of the *Jentung* arabesque and grape arabesque patterns. These three patterns are combined in some tiles which are hardly discernible from the two latter patterns. Compared with the *Jentung* and grape patterns, the floral medallion pattern is of a complicated design. The most outstanding among relics falling under this category were excavated in the remains of Sach'ŏn-wang and Punhwang temples.

The miscellaneous flower pattern contains the characteristics of the arabesque pattern but to a lesser degree. Many of the roof tiles with this pattern have a design of flowers and leaves placed loosely or of the same marks placed in a row.

(C) **The bird and beast pattern**—Patterns common to this category include waterfowls, birds, beasts, and such legendary animals as the dragon, phoenix and unicorn (the animal of good omen) peculiar to East Asia. Many of these patterns combined with those of clouds, rosaries or florae and some with animal-head patterns evolved from the so-called glutton motive (*t'ao-t'ieh wen*) of Yin and Chou of ancient China.

Among representative examples in this category is the so-called three-legged toad and hare pattern roof tile (originating from a legend of ancient China) which was unearthed from the site of Hwangnyong Temple in Kyŏngju and is now preserved in the Kyŏngju Museum. It is an exquisite objet d'art. Another example is a rarer specimen called the *kalavinka* pattern which consists of the body of a bird with a human face and arms, some in flight and others standing on the legs of a bird. The name *kalavinka* originated from that of an Indian bird reputed to have sung beautifully. The name of this bird came to Korea by way of China along with Buddhism. Examples of these roof tiles are found in the sites of such temples Pomun, Sach'ŏn-wang, and Hwangnyong in

Kyŏngju.

(D) **The flying patterns of birds and beasts**—The patterns of flying birds and beasts of good omen appear not only in roof tiles but the most beautiful are found in the flat tiles of the Unified Silla period. There are, however, such patterns as a phoenix flying in clouds or a dragon flying in the cloud of good omen. These roof tiles discovered in the sites of Ch'angnim Temple, Imhae-jŏn Pavilion, and a temple in Tongch'ŏn, Kyŏngju, have a band of rosaries around the rim.

(E) **The flying fairy patterns**—These are also found in the sites of such ancient temples as Hŭngbok. Pomun, and Sach'ŏn-wang and in Imhae-jŏn Pavilion in Kyŏngju and the figures common to all such roofing tiles consist of a pair of flying fairies playing musical instruments or carrying thuribles. These patterns are of Buddhist origin. The lines of the fluttering heavenly robes and of the cloud of good omen adrift between the robes yield a sense of rhythmic animation.

In addition to the above patterns in roof tiles, there are also such unusual patterns as the one which has the face of a Buddhist figure engraved in relief. For instance the one unearthed from the site of Hŭngyun in Kyŏngju has a smiling human face on a round tile. The figures in relief are most realistic and seem to have been made by delicate hands and not mass-produced from some original pattern. Fragments of such roof tiles were discovered around the site of Ch'angnim Temple, although it is impossible to locate their original site.

This roof tile with a Buddhist figure, formerly in the private collection of a Japanese named Takenosuke Okura, is now in

Tile with monster face, 7th—8th century

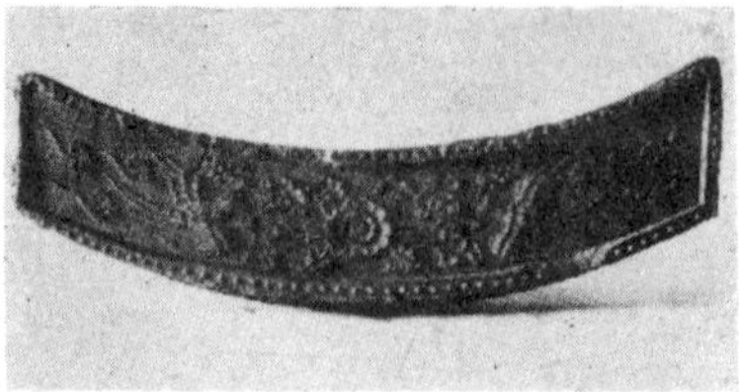

Birds and floral pattern tile

the Kyŏngju Museum. The Buddhist figure carved in relief shows a technical refinement that has overcome degrading elaborateness. Although it can be roughly estimated that it was made at the end of the Unified Silla period or Koryŏ dynasty, it is nevertheless an exceptional relic.

Monster and Falcon Decoration

Tiles depicting the face of a monster were used to decorate the roofs of palaces and temples during the Unified Silla period and accordingly have in recent years been unearthed from the sites of large ancient edifices. The tradition of decorating roofs with some tiles depicting the faces of monster in order to ward off evil persisted until the end of the Yi dynasty (1910). The origin of this tile goes back to the glutton motive found on the bronzeware of the Yin and Chou periods of ancient China. In the ancient China the glutton motive developed into the monster face pattern and thus was introduced to Silla. Such sculptural maturity and technical refinement have not been discovered in either T'ang China or in the Nara period of ancient Japan but is rather comparable to the sculptural art of ancient Rome. These tiles, though small, were artistic masterpieces indeed of which Silla craftsmen were justly proud.

Although the form of the monster tile varies according to usage, the pattern common to all is encircled with rosary-shaped *Jentung* arabesque or dot patterns. Some monster tiles were glazed green as the one excavated from the site of Sach'ŏn-wang Temple in Kyŏngju.

The falcon-head tile, a peculiar type of roofing tile used to decorate the ends of the ridge of the roof is larger and rarer than other types of tile. It is said that, although it is an Indian type of roofing tile introduced to Korea by way of China, the style originated in Assyria. It was introduced to T'ang China from the west (Asia Minor) along with the current of esoteric

Buddhism. The best tile of this type remaining known to have been made during the Unified Silla period was discovered on the site of a temple in Ch'ongun-ri, Kyŏngju, and is now preserved in the Kyŏngju Museum. It belongs to the T'ang period type. The basic pattern seems to be of feathers. However, it is neither a bird nor a fish but a graphic expression of some imaginary animal.

Floor Tiles and Bricks

In step with the refinement of the sculptural design of roofing tiles during the Unified Silla period, that era's flooring tiles and bricks are also unique in their design and technical excellence. Exquisite and delicate, they are well balanced. Some are superior to T'ang products in creativity and technique. As construction materials, the position flooring tiles and bricks occupy in art is very important in order to strike harmony with the design of roofing tiles of an edifice. The design of roofing tiles are visually less effective due to their lack of proximity to direct view, while the design of flooring tiles and bricks are more readily viewed. Hence flooring tiles and bricks were more endearing to the Silla people. Flooring tiles and bricks are classified into three categories according to use, namely, as flooring, for the decoration of inside walls, and as building materials.

Flooring Tiles—Designs common to flooring tiles consist of floral medallions, lotus-flower patterns, floral medallion-arabesque, and grape-arabesque patterns combined with bird and beast patterns. The origin of these designs is traced back to those excavated from ancient China, but the Chinese product is not as good as that of Silla in respect to versatility of design and technical refinement. The flooring tile is also classified into four categories according to use and design, namely, rectangular, diamond, oblong and triangular. The most representative are those unearthed from the site of Imhae-jŏn Pavilion in Kyŏngju and preserved in the Kyŏngju Museum. One of them, rectangular in shape, has the most exquisite floral-medallion design. Its surface is most delicately designed with the double-petalled, floral-medallion pattern in relief, and on each corner of the rectangle appears one quarter of the central floral-medallion design so that a combination of the same patterned flooring tiles produces a series of complete floral-medallion patterns on the floor. One of the more noticeable points about this flooring tile is that on one side exquisite arabesque patterns appear in relief while in the center of the pattern are two life-like deer in relief facing each other. One characteristic common to all the flooring tiles of the Unified Silla period is that their lines are so clear-cut as to look like knife blades, while the flow of the exquisite is matchless. Some flooring tiles are glazed in dark green, as is the case of one discovered at the site of Sach'ŏn-wang Temple in Kyŏngju.

The flooring tile that has exceptional design is the rectangular one discovered at the same site and preserved in the Kyŏngju Museum. The design is of a deva king sitting on the head of a devil. Such masterful handicraft designs demonstrate the graphic ability and creativity of the golden era of Silla art as do the stone sculptures in the Sŏkkuram Cave Temple at Kyŏngju.

Ceramic Wares Salvaged from the Seabed off Sinan

CHŎNG YANG-MO

An archeological investigation began in October 1976 off the coast of Sinan on a ship sunken off the southwestern tip of the Korean peninsula which is presumed to date back to the Yüan era. A preliminary survey was conducted in October and again in November that year. This was followed by the first major investigation in 1977 and the second one this year. In all, four investigations have been carried out.

It is, however, difficult to cover the whole range of the extensive investigations, the methods employed, and their academic results here since they were the first marine archeological attempts of their kind in this country and the sunken ship contained an enormous quantity of relics. I will, therefore, present only a brief explanation of the ceramic ware discovered in the vessel.

The ceramic items salvaged and examined up to August 12 this year break down to 6,435 celadons, 3,664 white porcelains and ch'ing-pai ware, 208 black-glazed wares (including Tenmoku), 155 wares coated with glazes made in imitation of the Chün Yao product, 5 wares with a pattern of black flowers on the white-glazed body, and 1,259 wares glazed black brown. Besides, some earthenware vessels were also found.

General Survey of Ceramic Wares

Celadons are most numerous among the many types of ceramic articles found; this enables us to presume that celadons formed the main current in ceramic vessels used in China until the Yüan era. The celadons salvaged from the bottom of the sea are presumed to have been produced at the Lung-ch'uan kiln in Chekiang Province and at kilns nearby which were in the sphere of influence of Lung-ch'uan. Besides, there are two or three celadon bottles which imitated products from South Sung's government-operated kilns and two celadon incense burners glazed greyish white and with cracks on the glaze which, too, fall under the type of government kiln products. Celadons are followed in number by white porcelains and ch'ing-pai ware. Most of them look like products of the Ching-te-chen kiln in Kiangsi Province. Others include ch'ing-pai ware manufactured at local kilns in Kiangsi, Chekiang, and Fukien Provinces. Included in the white porcelains is a considerable amount of ware that can be considered as Shu-fu products. Also included are three pieces of ware in the type of products of Ting Yao in Hopei Province, three other pieces glazed egg-white whose kiln and type cannot be identified, and some coarse and thick white porcelains and ch'ing-pai ware whose kilns and types cannot be traced. Found among the black-glazed vessels are many tenmoku tea-cups produced at the Chien Yao kiln in Fukien Province and small cups whose clay is coarse and colored beige, with a glaze colored dark brown or yellowish brown. Besides, there are pieces of ware whose clay is beige and whose glaze is black and coated thick and others whose bottom outside is coated with a yellowish brown glaze and whose surface is glazed black as in the former wares except the lines radiating vertically are painted in iron upon the glaze. Even though it is not clear at which kilns they were baked, the wares show a similarity to the so-called Kanan Tenmoku. Besides, we found brown-glazed small jars, which are believed to be products of the Chi-chou kiln. Most of them are small, but others are relatively large, some coated with the Chün Yao glaze and others glazed black.

Ware coated with glazes in imitation of the Chün Yao glaze comprise flowerpots, washbowls, and pot-shaped pitchers. Their glazes and clay are different from those of Yüan's Chün Yao ware of North China; and it is presumed that their glazes and clay were imitations of North China products made in South China. Compared with the northern products, their clay is coarse and they are coated double—with a black glaze and with lye upon it. Not one of them shows a tinge of red as an emanation of underglaze copper or the beautiful sky-blue hue. Among the five pieces which have a pattern of black flowers on the white-glazed body, one item—a small bottle—is believed to be a product of the Chi-chou kiln. The other four are considered to belong to the type of Tz'u-chou ware; but, as the Chi-chou kiln was influenced by the Tz'u-chou kiln, they, too, may be regarded as products of the Chi-chou kiln.

Celadons

The celadons, as explained earlier, are products of the Lung-ch'uan kiln and kilns in the sphere of its influence, most of them dating back to the Yüan period. Dishes and bowls hold numerical superiority in the celadons; but they also include vessels of various shapes such as large vases, large jars, small pots, and pitchers.

Among the dishes and bowls, those whose mouth is curved outward around the brim are larger in number than those whose mouth is upright. The glazes are colored mostly brown, yellowish brown, or olive. Their clay is mostly grey; but in some pieces the clay is more like that of white porcelains. Most commonly the patterns are carved in intaglio or in pressed relief. Found most commonly are pasted flowers and hieroglyphic designs, which are various and unrestrained. But in some vessels, the patterns are crude and clumsy. The handling of the supports is not uniform; and almost no ware shows the mark of sharp edging. Included are celadons with underglaze iron dots though they number only five or six. Compared with other celadons, they have a smooth surface; and their glaze is tinged with beautiful olive. Yüan celadons of this kind were discovered in Japan; and it is a noteworthy fact that they were discovered also in the Philippines. *Oriental Ceramics Discovered in the Philippines* (by Leandro and Cecilio Locsin) and the *Chinesische Keramik auf den Philippinen* report on the discovery of Yüan wares which, though lacking large vases and jars, did include small pitchers,

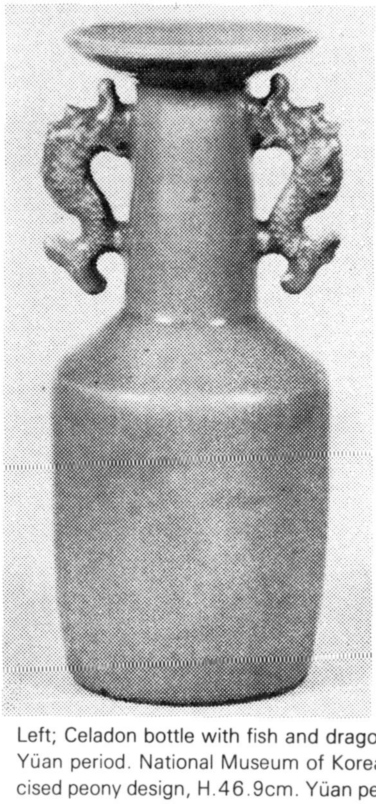

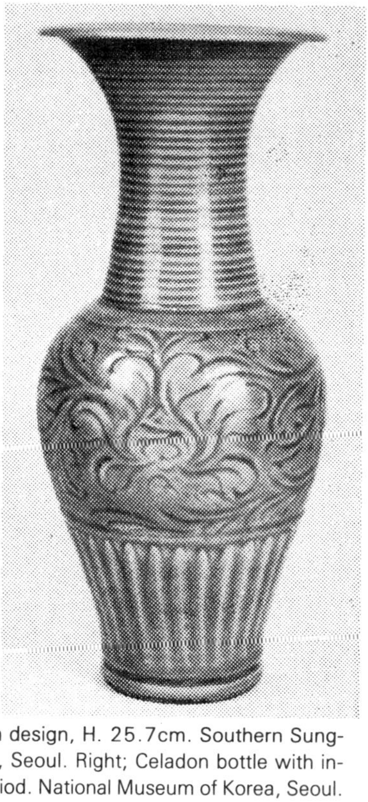

Left; Celadon bottle with fish and dragon design, H. 25.7cm. Southern Sung-Yüan period. National Museum of Korea, Seoul. Right; Celadon bottle with incised peony design, H.46.9cm. Yüan period. National Museum of Korea, Seoul.

small pots with ears, large trays, dishes, small cups, and incense burners, which are similar to the finds off Sinan in Korea. Of these, the discovery of small pitchers and small pots with ears was almost not reported elsewhere other than in the Philippines and Southeast Asia.

Also included are five or six celadons whose glaze is beautiful and whose shape is exact. They are of the grade of vessels which were once regarded as best ware from South Sung.

Most cups have an upright mouth; and their supports are treated with sharp edging, their soles are unglazed, being deep rustcolored or light brown. The glaze is coated thick, its colors ranging from deep green to light green. Most of them lack patterns. The cup-trays bear a clearly visible pattern of lotus flower petals carved in relief on the outer surface. They show a wide difference from a similar pattern which is accredited to Yüan potters. Other common patterns are pasted flowers and hieroglyphic designs. Much time was devoted to discussions on these two types of celadons at last year's domestic symposium in Korea on the ceramic wares salvaged from the seabed off Sinan; and I will refrain from going into detail here.

White Porcelains and Ch'ing-pai Ware

White porcelains and ch'ing-pai ware were discussed in the past with division into two different categories in some cases and without division in other cases by including the latter in the broad category of white porcelains. In some other cases, however, the division was not so distinct. For convenience's sake, they will be divided here into the Shu-fu type white porcelains, general white porcelains, and ch'ing-pai ware.

Various kinds of white porcelains were recovered from the bottom of the sea in Korea this time. First we are called on to discuss the Shu-fu white porcelains. Even though they do not bear the inscription of 樞府 (Shu-fu) or 福祿 (fu-lu), they are similar to ware which bears the inscription of Shu-fu in terms of shape and pattern and we can, instead, find inscriptions 玉[王?] (yu) or 正 (cheng) or an undecipherable inscription looking like Mongolian script on both sides of the upper part inside the vessels which are the very places where we find the inscription 樞府 in other wares. Compared with the ch'ing-pai ware, some of the Shu-fu ware has far more sharp-edged lines and others far softer lines and most of their patterns are carved in pressed relief and clearly visible. Their clay is hard; so is their glaze. They show no cracks on the glaze and are glazed on the entire surface except the soles of the supports. They show no mark of being baked in the overturned position; their supports are relatively large, giving an impression of stability. It is presumed that these white porcelains were produced immediately before the debut of the Shu-fu type ware or were used together with the Shu-fu porcelains briefly in the early years of their debut.

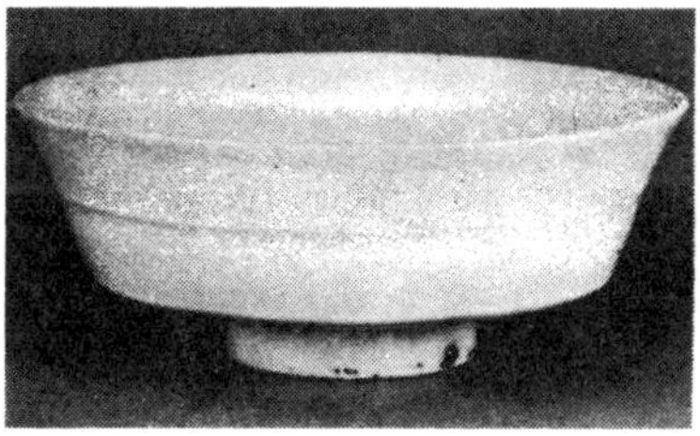

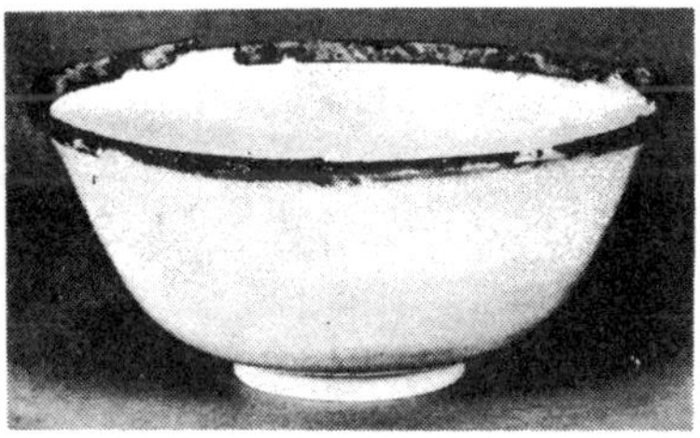

Left; White porcelain bowl, diameter at mouth 12.2cm. Yüan period. National Museum of Korea, Seoul. Right; Ch'ing-p'ai bowl with incised lotus and fish design, diameter at mouth 14.5cm. Yüan period. National Museum of Korea, Seoul.

Besides these good-quality white porcelains, we found coarse and different white porcelains. To be cited first are those which bear inscriptions 崑山玉出 (k'un-shan-yu-ch'u) 自然衣食 (tzu-jan-i-shih), or 福祿 (fu-lu) or patterns of plant leaves stamped in relief, all found on the bottom inside the vessels. Seen generally, they are tinged a little with beige and their supports and the area around them and the brims of their mouths are not glazed. They show no cracks on the glaze.

They are believed to have been baked in the overturned position. All the wares are framed gold invariably around the brim of the mouth. Their supports are large and look forceful. Ware similar to this type but about one century older was discovered in the Imazu Tomb in Japan. A discovery of similar ware was reported in Korea, too.

Second, there is a different group of white porcelains though they number only three. Their surface is colored deep egg-white or almost beige, show cracks, their glaze and clay are a little hard, the soles of their supports are unglazed, and the supports indicate that the ware underwent very clean treatment. Included among these is an incense burner. Attracting our attention is that the decoration mounted on this incense burner assuming the shape of a dragon head is just the same as the decoration on the large incense burner produced at the Chün Yao kiln and bearing the inscription 己酉 (chi-yu) which was excavated from the eastern outskirts of Huho-hao-te City in Inner Mongolia. Even though this utensil was treated with very delicate hands in terms of its shape and handling of its support, it is not clear at which kiln it was made.

Third, we found three large white porcelain dishes which are similar to the Ting Yao porcelains from Hopei Province. A thin glaze is coated on the entire surface except the brims of the mouths, which retain the mark that a gold frame was once affixed there. Visible inside are delicate and sharp patterns carved in relief. The walls are thin and the supports are cut cleanly. The supports retain the mark of being grasped by hands when the wares were glazed. Besides these there are several crude pieces whose walls are thick and whose supports and the area around them are not glazed.

Ch'ing-pai Ware

As explained above, there is some ch'ing-pai ware which is

difficult to distinguish from white porcelains because the overwhelming trend was in a process of switch over to hard white porcelains and ch'ing-pai ware was a product of this transitional period. I will classify the ch'ing-pai ware into three types including even those whose line of classification is very vague.

This first group is ware which everyone can easily identify as ch'ing-pai at first glance if one follows the conventional view. They are most numerous among the three. Dishes and soup bowls account for 90 per cent of the ch'ing-pai ware of this type, the rest being pillows, bottles, kettles, incense burners, jars, ink water droppers, and very small tableware as burial accessories. Of these, the dishes and soup bowls are a little coarse and large vessels such as bottles are of good quality. The dishes and bowls are thinly walled, their supports are small, and patterns pressed in relief cover the whole inside surface but they are not clear. In all the ware, the brim of the mouth is not glazed and encircled with a thin gold frame which has a certain width. Some have their supports glazed and others retain the mark of the glaze scrubbed off the supports. Some of the ch'ing-pai ware is very similar to the Shu-fu white porcelains in terms of shape; and an especially interesting point is that some of the ch'ing-pai dishes are decorated with a pattern of belt-like lines around the central part of the outer surface, a point that makes this group of vessels look almost similar to the Shu-fu white porcelains. There are many different points between ch'ing-pai ware and Shu-fu white porcelains. Some examples are as follows: Compared with the Shu-fu white porcelains, the ch'ing-pai ware has far smaller supports. Whereas the Shu-fu ware has no glaze on the soles and the inside surface of the supports, the ch'ing-pai ware is glazed there in most cases, some showing the mark of the glaze scrubbed off after it was coated. Whereas the Shu-fu ware is glazed up to the brim of the mouth, the ch'ing-pai ware is not glazed on the mouth part and all were baked in the overturned position. Also the Shu-fu ware is correct and refined in shape while the ch'ing-pai ware is less so.

Mixed with the ch'ing-pai vessels are some ware whose walls are a little thick and which are decorated with coarse patterns. Besides these ch'ing-pai dishes and soup bowls, we found large vessels which are far better in quality and glazed all over the surface except the soles and the inside part of the supports. Their patterns are various, including those engraved in intaglio, hieroglyphic designs, and those pressed in relief. Their shapes are also multifarious. Among small vessels such as ink water droppers, some were made by being cast into a mold. They include small flat ones and others assume the shape of a phoenix. They strikingly resemble ink water droppers found in the Philippines and other Southeast Asian countries. Included among the dishes, bowls, and other large vessels are some ware which is discolored black as a result of infiltration of carbon into the glaze in the course of firing inside the kiln, a case of failure to produce the effect of underglaze copper red.

In addition to dishes, soup bowls, bottles, and pots we examined above, there are very small articles. It is presumed that they were intended to serve burial or other ceremonial purposes rather than aimed at practical purposes. All of the small articles assume the shape of an incense burner or of a bottle, glazed all over the surface except the inside of the supports. Cast into a mold, they retain on both sides of the interior the mark of a joint which connected one mold with another at the time of casting. Small vessels of this kind were discovered on many occasions in the Southeast Asian region around the Philippines. There was no report on their discovery in other areas.

The second group embraces ch'ing-pai ware which is better than the first group in terms of the quality of the raw glaze, shape of vessels, and patterns. They are more thinly walled not only in the sides but even in the bottom, imparting the impression that they were as if half-transparent. The glaze is very smooth and tinged with light blue. Though thinly walled, these wares bear close resemblance to those which are decorated with a beaded pattern. They are glazed all over the surface except the brim of the mouth which is encircled with a thin gold frame which has a certain width. There are three types of bowls, all not glazed around the brim of the mouth and their supports beautiful and very small. Their patterns include a combination of lotus flowers and fish pressed in relief inside fine waves and various flowers. Some are not decorated with a pattern. It seems that these ch'ing-pai vessels, showing a remarkable improvement in comparison with ordinary ware, were produced for the special purpose of responding to demand from the royal household. It also seems that they represent the best of ch'ing-pai ware developed at the Ching-te-chen kiln. Compared with the first group, they are decorated with patterns which are more delicate and more distinct. Their patterns share some common points with some patterns of Yüan's ch'ing-pai ware, and it is presumed that there must have been some relations between the two.

The third group comprises ch'ing-pai ware which has something in common with the Shu-fu white porcelains and large-sized ch'ing-pai vessels in terms of quality. Ware of this type looks more akin to white porcelains. Their shapes include small gourd-shaped pitchers, small pitchers, ink water droppers in the shape of a shepherd-boy mounted on an ox, flower-shaped dishes, gourd-shaped vessels, and small bottles. They are relatively thinly walled, glazed all over the surface except the bottom and the support. The unglazed parts are left white. Included among the gourd-shaped pitchers and the ink water droppers in the shape of a shepherd-boy mounted on an ox are seven or eight items which are decorated with underglaze iron dots. Some of them were discovered for the first time; but most vessels of these types were discovered in Southeast Asia previously, except those with underglaze iron dots which were discovered only in the Philippines, according to Japan's Professor Tsuguo Mikami. This finding can be considered an important clue to finding out the ports this sunken vessel had called on before it came to the shores of Korea.

Black-Glazed Ware

This type of ware consists of Tenmoku and ordinary ware. Included in the Tenmoku type are pieces similar to the tea-cups baked at the Chien Yao kiln or to ware which is called Kanan Tenmoku. The Chien Yao tea-cups can be classified into three types according to the difference of the mouths. The three can again be classified into large and small ware. Two togo Tenmoku pieces, all encircled with a gold frame, were found inside a wooden box where they were kept from others. There are three or four strangely shaped tea-cups whose clay ranges in color from beige to blackish brown and whose sides are almost upright, their glaze being almost similar to the Chien Yao product.

Only one kind of ware similar to the Kanan Tenmoku had been found in the sunken ship until 1977, consisting of jars and bottles, whose clay is beige and coarse, whose glaze is pitch dark and lustrous, and whose lower parts including the supports are not glazed. Some of the ware was once coated with a brown glaze and then with a black glaze from above, with the result that the black glaze covers the whole surface or

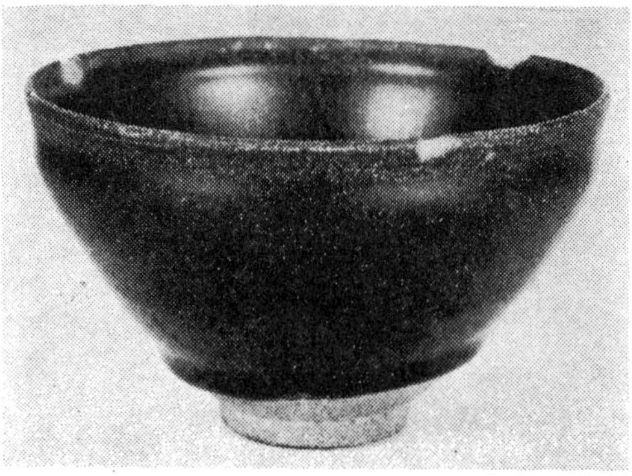

Black glazed bowl, D. at mouth 12.3cm, Southern Sung-Yüan period. National Museum of Korea, Seoul.

it spills down to the bottom. These kind of jars and bottles were discovered this year. They include those wares which are decorated with lines engraved on the glaze. In addition, bottles and soup bowls of other types were also found.

Almost all the soup bowls are coated with a black glaze in the lower part and coated over it again with the lustrous Tenmoku glaze from above. The iron lines are either straight in the form of radiant rays or short in duplication. Their clay is hard unlike the jars and beige resembling the clay of celadons.

Most numerous among the black-glazed ware found off Sinan are small cups which are coated with a blackish brown or dark brown glaze over a beige and slightly coarse clay. Their mouths are curved a little inward and the mark left by the wheel is noticeable on the rest of the surface. The supports are treated crudely, they are not glazed on the lower part. These cups were discovered only rarely in the Philippines but relatively frequently in Japan. It is presumed that there were many kilns for this black-glazed ware in Fukien, Kiangsi, and Kwangtung Provinces.

Also discovered were two slightly large cups which are different in the glaze and shape. They are coated with the celadon glaze or the white porcelain glaze only on the brim of the mouth.

There are many small bottles and small jars which come under a different category of black-glazed ware (some being similar to iron-glazed ware). The small bottles are as black and thick with glaze as the Tenmoku ware while the small jars are as rust-colored and thin with glaze like underglaze iron ware. Among the former, some are glazed all over the surface while others are not glazed on the lower parts. They are of several different shapes. The latter ware has only one shape, they are not glazed on the lower parts, and they are flat-bottomed, with the bottoms cut off with a thread. Many of the former type were discovered in Southeast Asia including the Philippines.

Besides these small pieces, more than 10 black-glazed large

jars with an ear in the four corners were salvaged, bearing the inscriptions 淸香 (ch'ing-hsiang), 天寶 (tiem-pao), and 寶 (pao) on the shoulder. The larger ones measure 60 centimeters in height; and their glaze is brown, blackish brown, or blackish brown mixed with purple. Many cases of discovery of these four-eared large jars have been reported in the Philippines and other South-east Asian countries.

In 1977 a score of celadon flowerpots were picked up from the sea. This year, however, only a few vessels of this type were salvaged, in addition to one black-glazed flowerpot which is exactly the same in shape as the celadon pot. It seems that the discovery of a celadon flowerpot is very rare throughout the world. Based on the assumption that the origin

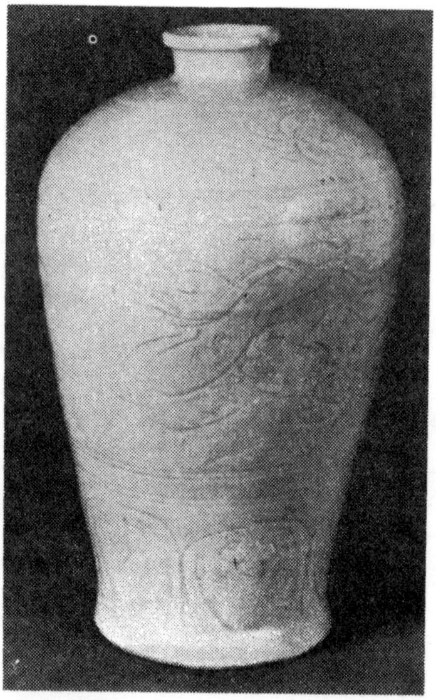

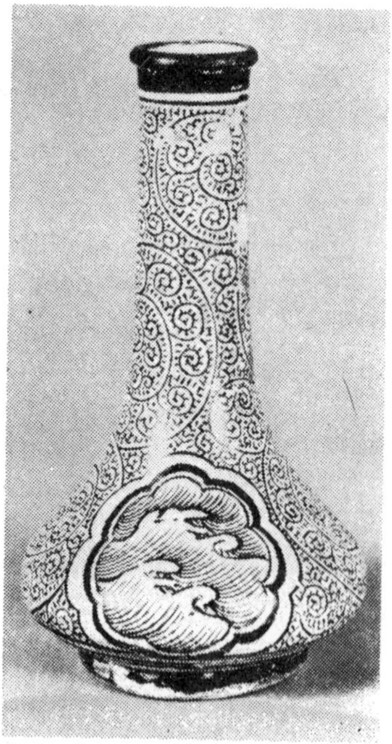

Left; Ch'ing-p'ai vase with incised dragon and cloud design, H. 26.8cm, Yüan period. National Museum of Korea, Seoul.
Right; Black glazed bottle with floral and arabesque design, H. 14.6cm. Yüan period. National Museum of Korea, Seoul.

of the celadon flowerpots was the Lung-ch'uan kiln, we may presume that the black-glazed flowerpot was also made at the same kiln.

There are strangely shaped jars which, though looking like black-glazed ware, are coated with a beautiful and brownish glaze only on the inside and the glaze on whose outside surface was cleanly scrubbed off after glazing. The entire surface is decorated with concentric ellipses in intaglio and raised dots surround the neck. The raised dots are coated with a white (light blue) glaze. These strangely shaped small and large jars, numbering more than 10, are of the same shape but can be classified into three types by kind of glaze. But the type described above is most representative.

Another type has the whole surface, both inside and outside, glazed pitch dark except the outside bottom. There are no decorative lines carved in intaglio, and there are lines of raised dots around the neck, the dots glazed white. Another type has glaze coated on the outside surface and subsequently scrubbed off after the ware was coated entirely, both inside and outside, with the raised dots around the neck retaining the glaze. Lines are carved in intaglio on the whole surface.

Ware with Chün Yao Style Glaze

Flowerpots are most numerous among ware of this type, followed in order by washbasins and pot shaped pitchers, the latter numbering only a few. The very coarse clay mixed with iron and impurities was first coated with a dark brown glaze and then with a greyish blue lye. Its surface color is blue mixed with grey and purple and there is no red as an emanation of underglaze copper. The lower parts such as the supports are not glazed. It is presumed that this ware was made in southern China under the influence of the Chun Yao in Hopei Province which had spread southward. There is a wide difference from the products of Yüan's Chün Yao kiln.

Ware with Underglaze Iron-black Decoration

Ware of this type comprises two jars, one bottle, and two lids. Presumed in all the three kinds is that a coarse clay was coated first with a white glaze and then the pattern was drawn with iron on the white glaze or that the clay itself was white tinged slightly with beige. It is not clear, however, which is the more probable presumption. One bottle among them shows an arabesque pattern on the whole surface, with both corners of the trunk reserved for pictures, one showing a branch of a flower plant and the other a pattern of waves. A piece exactly the same as this one was once discovered in Nanchang, Kiangsi Province. As the Nanchang ware has a pattern which is exactly the same as that of the bottle found in Sinan, it can be presumed that the latter was made at the Chi-chou kiln. Also presumed is that other ware, too, were products of the Chi-chou kiln even though they show some characteristics of the Tz'u-chou ware.

Ware with Black-Brown Glaze

These wares are made of a clay which, though coarse, is strongly fire-resistant and which was coated with a glaze which contained a considerable amount of iron. It is presumed that they were made as containers for tea or other foodstuffs. They are of three different shapes. One type has four ears and others do not have them. Those without ears can be classified into slender ware and slightly plump ware. In quality, those which are slender, whether they are furnished with ears or not, are more solid. Jars of this type were once found in Korea and frequently in Japan; but in the Philippines and other Southeast Asian countries, their discovery was far less frequent.

Earthenware

The earthenware comprises large jars with four ears and figurines painted black. The large jars with four ears are thinly walled and made of a coarse clay; presumably they were made to contain food. The figurines are hollow, with holes on the bottom. They contain something solid, for they give out sound when they are shaken.

Miscellaneous Ceramics

The miscellaneous ware is almost entirely Chinese; only four Korean and Japanese products are included here. The Korean articles comprise a mei-p'ing vase, a bowl, and a cup-tray. The celadon mei-p'ing vase with an arabesque pattern is presumed to date back to the first half of the 12th century, the celadon bowl with an inlaid pattern of clouds and cranes to the mid-12th century, and the celadon cup-tray with an inlaid arabesque pattern to the first half of the 13th century. The only Japanese article found in the ship is a setoyaki celadon-like mei-p'ing vase with a stamped pattern of peony; the glaze has mostly fallen off.

Questions of Dating

Answers to questions concerning dating and identity of kilns need to be withheld until the investigation of the relics contained in the sunken ship is brought to completion. Discussions took place at the domestic symposium held in Korea in 1977 concerning the question of dating; and I will mention it briefly here.

More than one million Chinese coins of various kinds have been taken up from the sea and they report that many are still buried at the bottom of the boat.

Our examination disclosed that there are 53 kinds of coins, the youngest are the Chih-ta-tsun-pao coins (minted in 1310). With this, we can safely fix the possible oldest age of the relics at 1310. As not one of the Chih-cheng-tsun-pao coins (minted in 1350), the second mintage during the Yüan era, was found, we can also fix the possible youngest age of the relics at 1349.

The fact that there was neither one white porcelain with underglaze blue nor one white porcelain with underglaze copper red included among the more than 3,600 ch'ing-pai ware and white porcelains, it is presumed that they were produced before the art of blue or red underglazing was developed.

Among the three pieces of lacquerware salvaged in 1978, one bears the inscription 辛未兮塘陳萬一叔造 written in red on the dark brown body. The year of sinmi (辛未) was either 1271 or 1331, but we have no means of saying for sure which one is correct. If it was 1331, then we can fix the possible oldest age at 1331.

Lacquer Ware and Ornaments

CH'OE SUN-U

Lacquerware

The lacquering technique was first developed in ancient China. Many elaborate pieces of lacquerware have been excavated from Korean soil, particularly noteworthy being those from The Tomb of the Painted Basket which date from the first or second century A.D. Although most of the themes are Confucian, some work indicates that native craftsmen were already acquiring remarkable skill from the Chinese overlords of this colony on Korean soil.

During the 1920s lacquered cups and paintings were unearthed from Silla tombs in Kyŏngju which demonstrated the remarkable craftsmanship attained in the fifth and sixth century. According to a history of this period, a government shop existed manufacturing lacquerware. Probably this dealt in lacquerware inlaid with mother-of-pearl, a technique then practiced by T'ang China with which Silla had close relations. One copper mirror has survived which shows this delicate technique.

However, by the Koryŏ period many examples of mother-of-pearl inlay exist as well as ordinary lacquerware. In 1272 the government established a special shop to mass-produce lacquered boxes with mother-of-pearl for safekeeping Buddhist scriptures.

Major pieces of this technique which have survived to this day include a perfume box decorated with willows and birds, a jar and a tray with arabesque designs, all kept at the Seoul

National Museum. There also exists a Buddhist scripture box with arabesque designs in the Tokugawa Art Museum of Nagoya, Japan, and a Buddhist rosary case with a tortoise design at Toma-ji as well as a tortoise-designed tray at Keishun-in. Besides these examples in Japan, there are other specimens abroad such as the British Museum's scripture box and one at Colongne's Oriental Museum and others in the United States and the Netherlands.

Most pieces of Koryŏ-period lacquerware extant are decorated with arabesque and chrysanthemum designs, which are similar to those found on the celadon made during the same twelfth and thirteenth centuries. This type of mother-of-pearl inlay in lacquerware would seem to have influenced the development of inlaid celadons, one of the chief glories of Koryŏ art. Towards the end of the dynasty, during the fourteenth century, this technique of mother-of-pearl inlay became less detailed and looser, declining as it lost its elaborateness, just as happened with inlaid celadons.

Early Yi dynasty lacquerware continued Koryŏ designs, with less use of tin and bronze wire and painted transparent tortoise designs. This later lacquerware is marked by the use of cattle bone powder or shell powder in black lacquer. Koryŏ's lacquerware with symmetrical designs gave way to simpler, plainer designs of flowers, birds and the four gracious plants—orchid, bamboo, chrysanthemum and plum. A gradual evolution occurred as described below:

During the fifteenth and sixteenth centuries, designs are boldly schematized lotus arabesque and imaginary Buddhist flowers, looser forms of the Koryŏ designs, appearing larger in size.

During the seventeenth and eighteenth centuries, designs such as two phoenix, two dragons or a bunch of grapes lost popularity, while the four gracious plants, flowers and birds increased in use, both on lacquerware and on the white porcelain of this period.

By the nineteenth century, designs depicting nature in a

more realistic manner had become popular. The usual theme encompasses the ten symbols of longevity—the sun, mountains, water, rocks, clouds, pine trees, the herb of immortality, tortoises, cranes and deer—amidst natural scenes painted in a light vein.

Ox-Horn Inlay

The technique of inlaying painted transparent ox-horn on the surface of woodwork is a craft unique to Korea. In general, Korean handicrafts are characterized by plain color and simple form, but ox-horn decorated works use bright colors in a variety of ways. Although the Korean people love plain colors, especially white, they use bold colors for the apparel of women and children. The history of ox-horn decoration can be traced back very early, since an ox-horn decorated needle-ruler a horizontal container has been found at the Shosoin Collection, which dates from 756 A.D. This includes the furniture of Japan's Emperor Shomu which was dedicated to the Buddhist temple of Todai-ji, Nara. It contained many imported wares, including some from Korea.

This technique of inlaying painted transparent ox-horn probably developed under the influence of China where they drew pictures on the back side of transparent material which results in seeing the pictures through the other side.

In Korea horns of young oxen are dipped into boiling water to remove the cartilage; then they are sliced into thin, transparent plates. Pictures are drawn on the back side of the plate with paints mixed with glue in order to later affix them to the woodwork surface. Such woodwork saw phenomenal development during the Yi dynasty. The most favored designs during this period represent the ten symbols of longevity. The principal colors are black, white, red, yellow, green and blue. Horn decoration was employed on spools, needle-rulers, combs, pillow ends, writing brushes, fans, knives, and stationery cases as well as on chests of drawers, thread boxes, dressing tables and jewelry boxes.

Chest Insignias

Chest insignias are those signs of rank worn on official dress both in China and Korea. They are embroidered on both the front and the back of the costume. Korea first established this system of chest insignia in 1485. During the Yi dynasty the highest rank insignia was a peacock, next came the wild goose, then a white pheasant for civilian officials. As for military officers, the first and second rank were indicated by a tiger and the third by a bear. Princes rated a giraffe, and the system went on down.

Changes did occur. For example, in the late nineteenth century a crane came to be used uniformly for all civilian officials and a tiger for those with military rank, a greater number of them indicating higher status. As the main designs of insignia changed, so did the background. In the early Yi period, peonies and clouds formed the background, but only clouds were used in the latter half of the sixteenth century. By the eighteenth century designs of waves, rocks and the *pulloch'o* or herb of immortality had been added to the cloud design.

Colors of chest insignia also changed with the passage of time. During the fifteenth and sixteenth centuries, orange formed the main background color, upon which were stitched designs in red, and green, which resulted in a poor color contrast (between design and background). By the seventeenth century the background color had become green, and the designs were in fresh, clear colors, with their borders in white in order to separate clearly the design from the background.

Yi dynasty insignias are embroidered horizontally, vertically and obliquely, expressing the designs with thin threads, bordered by thick, twisted threads. Gold and silver threads are also used, mixed with ordinary colors.

Ornamental Hairpins and Accessories

The oldest known ornaments of Korea are crowns, earrings, rings and gold and silver articles such as necklaces, belts and hairpins, all unearthed from the tombs of the Three Kingdoms period. These hold a unique place in ancient Asian culture. The styles of these ornaments are unique to Korea, except for the belts which are in China's Six Dynasties period manner. Korea's unique tradition of ornaments evolved in a variety of styles until the end of the Yi dynasty.

The ornaments worn by Yi dynasty women, such as hairpins, earrings, accessories and rings are distinctly different from those of Chinese and Japanese women. The style of their hairdo influenced these accessories. King Yŏngjo's order of 1756 that upper-class women must wear headgear, rather than waste money on wigs, also promoted this form. Although early hairpins were of tin, bronze and other inexpensive materials, later gold, silver and jade hairpins became popular. Silver hairpins decorated with one or more of the seven precious metals and stones (gold, silver, glass, marble, granite, jade and coral) were greatly loved by Yi dynasty women. White jade hairpins were also popular, decorated with various designs such as plum blossoms. Blue jade hairpins were even more precious and worn by wives of high ranking government officials and court women.

In addition, hairpins were fabricated from coral, yellow jade, buffalo horn, bamboo, tin and gold. Only a few gold hairpins have survived; tin hairpins are believed to have been used as a substitute for silver ones.

Hairpins were an important item of the family treasure, handed down from generation to generation during the Yi period. When decorated with the dragon and phoenix design they were worn only in a solemn ceremony. With the passage of time, hairpins became shorter in length and simpler in form.

The traditional costume of Korean women is embellished with various accessories made of gold, silver and jade. They are usually attached to the coat and on rare occasions they are also put on the upper part of the skirt. The origin for this can be found in articles unearthed from the tombs of the fifth and sixth centuries in Silla. The more immediate origin is, of course, accessories worn by Koryŏ dynasty court women. According to one record, twelfth century women wore a perfume case and other accessories on their clothes. A portrait of women by the eighteenth century painter Shin Yun-bok shows accessories, revealing that Yi dynasty women loved such ornaments. Originally they were for ceremonial court use, but began to be worn by upper-class women and later by lower-class women, not just for ceremony but also on ordinary clothes. They displayed a main and a secondary decoration which attached the former to the robe. Designs symbolized such things as wealth and rank, many sons, long life and happiness, health, chastity and exorcism. For example, the tiger's claw implies exorcism while the bamboo and plum designs and the ornamental knife symbolized chastity of women.

Traditional Patterns of Korea

SIN YŎNG-HUN

We still do not know sufficiently well the patterns engraved on rock surfaces, earthenware, woodenware and innumerable other daily utensils our ancestors fashioned in the course of a long history, nor do we know the aesthetic motifs of these patterns and the cultural background from which they derived. But we know that people preferred to decorate their utensils rather than produce items bare of patterns. So diverse, indeed, are the patterns that none of them are identical with one another.

This diversity of patterns may suggest that our ancestors had a disposition very sensitive to changes in appearance, a disposition which seems to have been cultivated by their inner urge rather than their simply aesthetic sensibilities. Again, we do not know the nature of their inner urge, and effort should be made to probe into it. As part of such effort, we have been collecting these patterns and attempting to bring some kind of order to them, so that they may reveal their real nature little by little.

We do not know how they come into being, how they spread and found their way into daily utensils, nor their function, nor their meaning as decorative elements. We have been collecting these patterns during the past decade, and sometimes encountered a huge cache of patterns which differed from one another in character, shape, period, usage, material and style. In that case it is very difficult to read the meaning of the patterns on the spot. The ordinary person pays attention to the most beautiful ones, but the student of archaeology and the history of art will be most interested in the oldest among them, while those not shapely in form and made in recent years will receive less and later attention.

This is the usual starting point, and from there some go to crude patterns and others from old to recent ones. If one frees himself from his preoccupation with the oldest and the most sophisticated, and traverses between the two extremes, one may be able to find what he has been seeking in the simple and crude patterns. Oftentimes one may be able to conjecture on the basis of recent designs the nature of older ones. Even the cruder example will reveal, if one looks into them with care and attention, information which is surprising and at the same time educational.

Classification of materials collected is no easy task, either. Some may be unique and others may belong to several or more categories. There are those who have classified these patterns according to shape, such as animal, plant, geometric, and literal; and others like beast, fowl, insect, flower, tree, lineal, lattice, lightning, sky and ghost patterns. Some have studied the origin and development of patterns such as the tortoise, and scholars of Korea, Japan and China have done comparative studies on the similarities and dissimilarities of patterns found in all three countries.

When the number of patterns under study was limited, attempts were made to classify and study them, but when the number exceeds tens of thousands, these attempts wound up

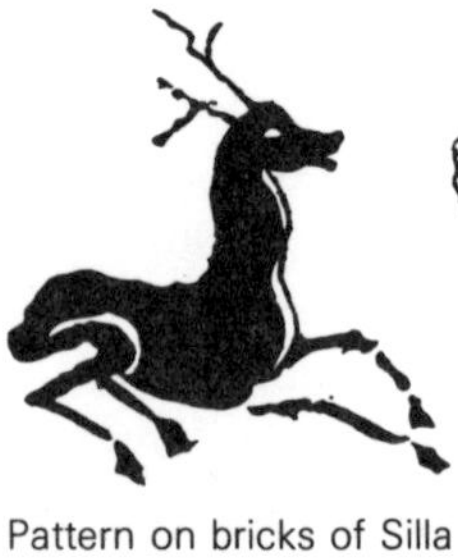

Pattern on bricks of Silla

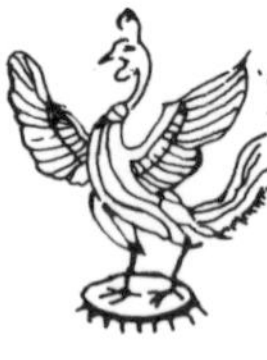

Mural at tomb No. 17 of T'ungkou, Koguryŏ

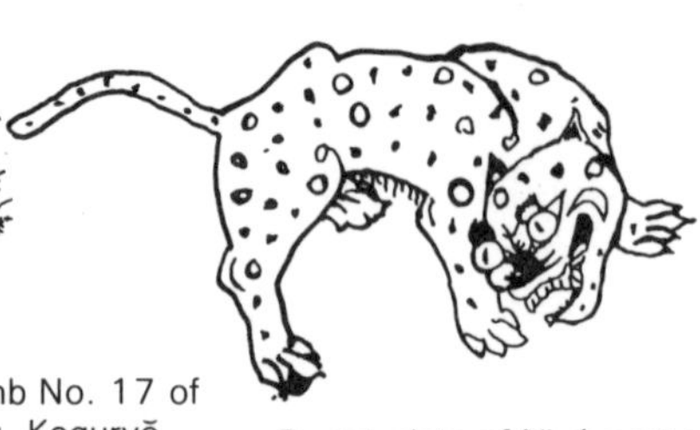

Breast-plate of Yi dynasty

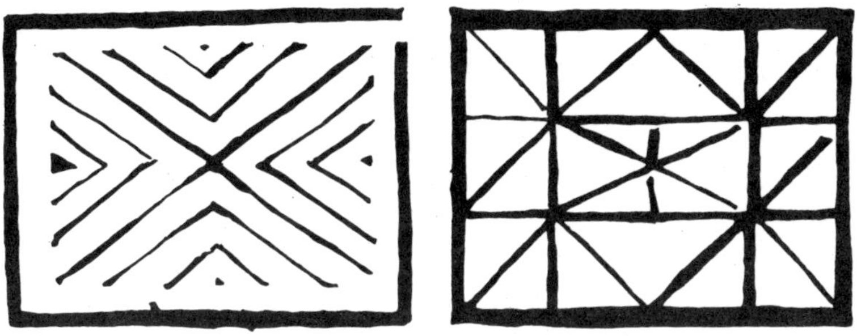

Wooden rice-cake mold of Yi dynasty

nowhere. The patterns of the rice-cake mold are such. No single item has such a diversity of patterns which defy classification. It is equally difficult to read the patterns engraved, especially on those made of celadon. The patterns engraved within a circle are highly symbolic or abstract, and the expression is so bold and fantastic that they deny access to the novice.

The rice-cake mold was first made of wood, and unlike the patterns on the celadon type, the patterns on the wooden ones are composed of compound designs. In such a diversity of patterns, one may come across very ancient motifs which can be found nowhere else but in the wooden rice-cake mold; for example, patterns found only in the earthenware and roof tiles of the Three Kingdoms period. The prehistoric line drawings and rock paintings of the Silla period maintain their life through the patterns of these rice-cake molds. It is pure coincidence that ancient and premodern engravers produced patterns identical with each other, which, on the other hand, suggests the fact that, even though they lived in different ages, they might have similar dispositions as regards the creation and reaction to identical patterns.

It may be said again that in this identity we may find an inner urge which they had in common, and which gave expression to identical manifestations. The problem is, then, what is this inner urge?

Recently a group known as the Folkist Society launched several joint research programs. Members of the society, about 150, collect materials needed for their own major field of study, and at times collect materials needed for common study projects. Jointly they can accomplish what usually takes a lifetime for an individual.

Patterns are not limited to a certain category; they appear on earthenware and ceramics, metal work, wooden articles, paper, leather and bamboo items and lacquerware, paintings and sculpture. Therefore there is virtually no limit to their use. Sometimes the patterns used in decorating Buddhist ceremonial articles found their way into those of Confucianism, into everyday life of the common people, and even the royal court.

As a means of condensing problems concerning classification and appraisal of artistic and philosophical implications, members of the Folkist Society have been publishing articles and academic papers through their journal *The Folkist*, through dissertations by student members of the society, and other journals such as this. The research and publication program will be continued until the projected Compendium of Korean Patterns is published.

According to an article on "Rice-Cake Models" published in the first volume of *The Folkist*, the patterns of the rice-cake molds have direct connection with man's desires and aspirations. This view has found an echo in Mr. Zo Za-yong's monograph on the art of the Korean people and his "Shamanistic Art of Korea" which was serialized in the *Sisa Graph* magazine.

For example, Mr. Zo views the patterns of parallel lines on the rice-cake impress as symbols of longevity and sharing of the years happily together between husband and wife, represented by the long noodles which ancient Koreans prepared for special occasions such as the first birthday or the wedding ceremony. And the oblique lattice patterns, commonly called gridiron patterns, he views as an implication of exorcism. He claims that such an implication is also found in the oblique lattice patterns of the corner roof tile of the Silla period, equivalent to what is called the roof tile with demon face, the demon face being meant to scare away evil.

This oblique lattice pattern is so widely utilized that it may be found in virtually all household items, and even in the shaman's amulet.

From the above it is noted that the oblique lattice pattern is an expression of man's certain desire, which may have some implication of the nation-founding myth of Tan'gun as recorded in the *Samguk Yusa*, in which it is written that Hwan'in, the Heavenly King, gave a set of three Heavenly Seals or Treasures to his young son, Hwan'ung, with which to rule over his people. These heavenly seals were believed to be symbols of the spirit of a clan society, and at the same to have the magic power to expel evil. These three took the form of a black horse, a round straw rope, and a javelin in Mongolia; and in Japan a mirror, a sword and beads.

Although we still do not know what these three heavenly seals are made of, we may be able to trace the origin of patterns in these things. And since they have something to do with heavenly things and the power to expel evil, they must have contained some designs or configurations that suggest the history of the Creation or symbols of magic power.

Returning to the *Samguk Yusa* again, since no one had ever met the ministers of wind, rain and clouds, the Heavenly King sent them to earth along with his son. The encounter with them or their ruling over the earth must have been expressed in one form or another by means of a certain form or configuration, and each must have been represented in a form peculiar to itself and different from others. Thus the representation of these elements of nature must have taken different forms, evolved from simpler to more complex ones. Here by representation is meant that of a pattern or configuration, and by evolution is meant that of design.

Early men must have expressed the idea or gesture of prayer

for rain, for a son and for happiness, and then moved in a positive direction, i.e., prayer for longevity, wealth and nobility, prolific offspring and expelling of evils. According to such a change of men's attitude, they were able to give expression to things tangible and intangible, in either a passive or positive way.

Since the prehistoric godlike human beings described in the *Samguk Yusa* descended to the tops of mountains, there naturally arose a belief in the high mountains as home of the mountain spirit. Thus the mountain and its spirit became intermediary between men and the elements of nature, i.e., wind, rain and clouds. And this intermediary became the indirect representation of the elements. From this might have been derived the designs of Buddhist sculpture and paintings, and what is called the "painting of mountain spirits." As an indirect method, the messenger was invented and the animals were personified under the name of "four gods" or "four spirits." And since the shaman presided over the sacrificial offerings as chief priest and head of the clan, the designs and configurations made for this purpose may be said to be those of Shamanism.

These shamanistic designs or configurations have been kept alive through prehistoric rock-carvings, ancient pottery, down to rice-cake molds. Alien patterns were introduced to Korea

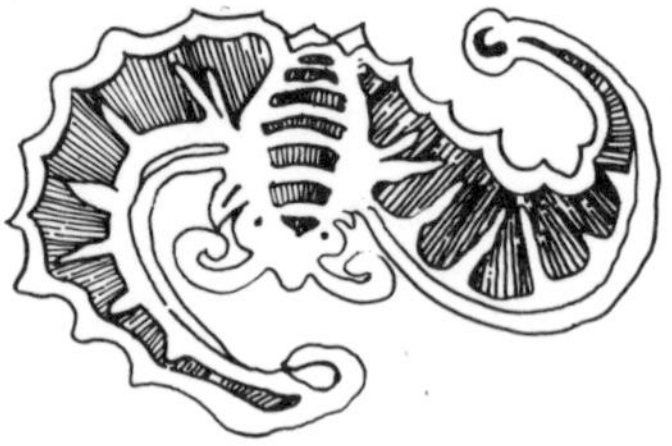

Butterfly pattern of Yi dynasty

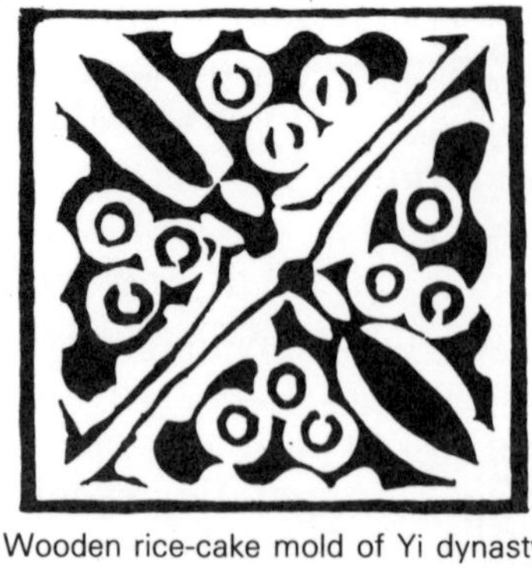

Wooden rice-cake mold of Yi dynasty

which, in the course of assimilation and adaptation, were also incorporated into Korean shamanistic patterns. The above process may be compared to the fact that, although Korea had been under the influence of Chinese culture since the importation of Chinese characters, except for a small minority of the ruling upper classes, the majority of the people had little to do with Chinese; they did not wear Chinese clothes, eat Chinese food, build Chinese-style houses, or speak the Chinese language. The same may be true in the case of Korean Buddhism, which came to have elements alien to Indian Buddhism, such as the Taoist shrine consecrated to the Big Dipper (Ch'ilsŏng-gak) and the shrine of the mountain spirit (Sansin-gak).

The reason why we place such a high importance on the patterns carved on the rice-cake mold is that we can compare some of the rice-cake mold patterns with prehistoric rock carvings recently discovered in Ŏnyang; and the comparison made it possible to read some meanings of the rock carvings. Especially the ⊕ pattern in the rock carving drew our attention, because it seems to have been related to the same pattern on the rice-cake mold and the corner roof tile of ancient times.

⊕ patterns have been proved, through materials collected from abroad by foreign members of the Folkist Society, almost universal throughout the world, along with patterns such as  and 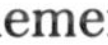, patterns which have so far been thought peculiar to Korea. It is like the prehistoric men who made stone implements. They were not influenced by neighboring tribes. It was a natural development. The forms and features of these patterns therefore may not be influenced by a more advanced neighboring society, even in prehistoric times. They were rather spontaneous manifestations by which human beings tried to give expression to their primordial urge.

What that primordial urge is will be revealed through continued effort. Instead of limiting the area of study to a certain region or a country, materials must be collected throughout the world, and must be brought together for comparative study. The more materials we have at hand, the easier it will become to shed light on them.

The patterns of Korea have many elements that may be seen as an extension of nature. The basic elements of a pattern are composed of dots and lines. But the line in this case is not taken as an extension of dots, but a pattern which has no beginning or end, as Mr. Zo said, and which therefore represented heaven and the earth, because the two are taken as endless. The straight lines of heaven and earth are parallel lines; the two lines, however, constitute a zone which helps define the inside and outside of a line, and sometimes male and female.

Heaven is thought of as round, which is common to all mankind. The Chinese called it the "circle of heaven." On the other hand, the earth is considered angular. The circle and angular square may contain smaller inner circles and inner squares, and may be contained by large outer circles and squares. And there may be a variety of circles and squares. The circle is thought of not as linking the two ends of a line, but rather as an expression of that which has neither beginning nor end. In this case the circle took the form of ◎ and in the case of the square, ⧈.

Between the parallel lines of heaven and earth, the

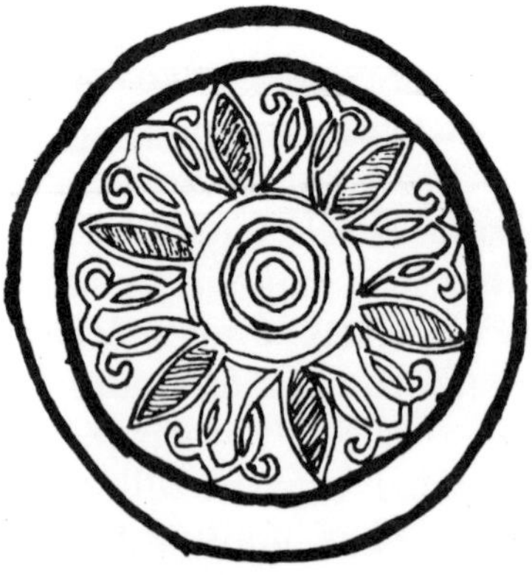

Concave roof-tile of Koguryŏ

mountain and human figure appeared as representations of Shamanism. The mountain sometimes was abstracted into the form of a triangle, and the human figure into a dot, or a string of beads or vertical line. In this way, the ministers of wind, rain and clouds took imaginary forms: the wind in horizontally moving lines; the rain in vertical lines, and the cloud in a slanting line. Thus vertical, horizontal and slanting lines fill the space between the parallel lines.

Human beings began to give expression, according to their predilections, to the object of worship such as the sun and moon and stars, rivers, trees, flowers, rocks, beasts and insects, and then pictorial symbols which served as the intermediary in their conversation with heaven, which is usually represented by such imaginary animals as a three-legged bird, dragon, dragon-horse, tortoise, and so forth. In this stage the symbolic animals are given concrete forms so that it is not difficult to understand their functions.

Shamanism is a petrified form of primitive beliefs, and accordingly its symbolic representation was fossilized, thus losing its persuasive power. When the more advanced religions of the world were introduced to Korea, Shamanism tried to go along with the theory of alien religions, and the alien religions relied on Shamanism as a means of taking root in foreign soil. In this process the alien religion assimilated some elements of Shamanism, and in the end the foreign religion would be left with only its theorized rituals, and its essence was incorporated into Shamanism.

Thus came into being such anomalies as Buddhist Shamanism, Taoist Shamanism, and Confucian Shamanism. A concrete example may be found in the attire of the mountain spirit in the shrine of the mountain spirit at Buddhist temples. At times when Buddhism was prevailing, the mountain spirit was clothed like a Buddhist figure, but wore Taoist dress when Taoism was in vogue, and Confucian dress when Confucianism was the ruling ideology. However, no change is discernible in the hoary seated figure and attendant tigers.

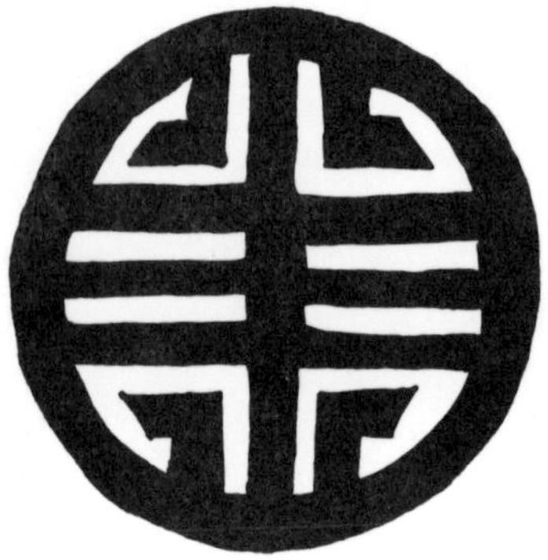
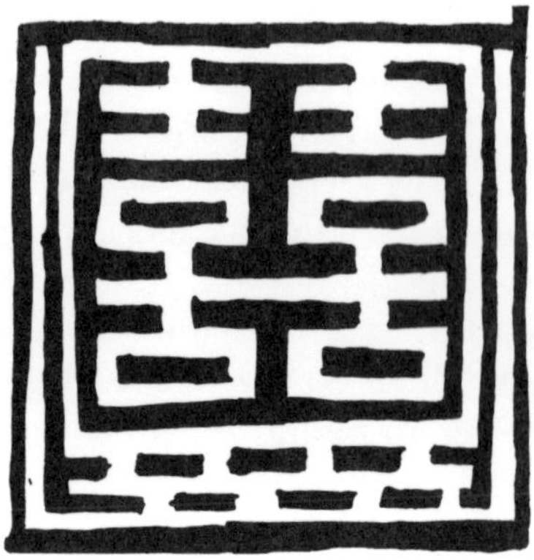

Wooden rice-cake molds of Yi dynasty

Silla painter Solgŏ is reputed to have drawn more than one thousand portraits, but none descended to posterity. But cannot we assume that the portrait of Tan'gun might have been the model from which the present day portraits of mountain spirits derived?

Patterns are conceived and composed out of this process and content. Those which became designated national treasures and appreciated were not made with such premeditated aims, but as daily necessities and out of the religious consciousness of the ancient people. To impress patterns on a piece of rice-cake was not motivated by the quest for the beautiful, but as an expression of prayer, with the hope that it might serve as a magic blessing or malediction.

The patterns reproduced in these pages number a little more than one hundred, and they are selected so randomly from among many that as a whole they will not serve the purpose of systematic classification or chronological development of patterns. To make the beginner's access to them smoother and easier, the patterns are selected from familiar handicraft works.

As briefly mentioned, many are engaged in the compilation of the Compendium of Korean Patterns. The names of researchers and their subjects are given in the following as a future reference: Kim Kyŏng-suk on the patterns of rice-cake molds; Kim Yong-ja on the Ten Everlasting Ones; Kim Chae-yong on the silver thread inlaid patterns; Kim Chin-suk on the tortoise patterns; Pak Kye-suk on the hairpin and its design; U Su-in on the dragon patterns; Yi Og-yong on the patterns of Buddhist temple bells; Chŏn Yong-ju on the patterns on locks; Ch'oe Chŏng-ja on the patterns of waves. When these researches are completed and published in a book, more detailed studies will be undertaken.

Many have completed or are in the process of completing research: Pak Yong-jin on the Paekche roof tiles and floor tiles; the Paekche Research Institute at Ch'ungnam University on the lineage of Paekche tiles; Kyoto University on the lineage of old tiles of Silla; Hwang Su-yŏng on the incense burner; Kim Hwa-yŏng on the lotus flower patterns; Im Yong-ju on the patterns on pottery; Yi Chun-gu on the water chestnut flower patterns; Chŏng Yong-ho on bronze bells; Kim Hŭi-jin on the embroidered pillow ends; Yi Chong-sŏk on handicraft patterns; Sin Yŏng-hun and Kim Tong-hyŏn on architecture; Yu Mun-yɔng on the Tanch'ŏng (many colors and designs); Im Tong-bin on seals; Yi Pae-gŭn on bronze mirrors; and Zo Za-yong on the tiger, mountain spirit, exorcism, longevity and happiness, and other good omens.

Symbolism in Traditional Korean Silk Designs

KWŎN YUN-HŬI

Up to the turn of the twentieth century, Korean arts were much influenced by China due to her close contact with China. Korea's tributary relationship with China started in the early part of the Yi dynasty (1392-1910 A.D.), and by the middle of the sixteenth century, the system had become highly systematized. Korean kings of the Yi dynasty annually sent Korean embassies with tribute to the Ch'ing emperor. The tribute included gold, silver, various sizes of paper, leopard skins, otter skins, deer skins, thin silk in various colors, cotton and hemp goods and rice among other items.[1] Gifts from the Ch'ing emperor to the King of Korea were sent in return for the tributary items. They were satin costumes for the king of Korea, various satin pieces, marten (pelts), and saddle horses. Korean embassies also received imperial gifts from the Ch'ing emperor, including a large proportion of satin goods (costumes and small satin pieces), silks, silver (in taels), blue cotton cloth pieces, and horses.[2]

In addition to this tributary relationship, Korea and China traded continuously during these periods. The trade was conducted in the Peking residence of the Korean embassy and was also officially permitted by the Ch'ing government. Many luxury items such as satins, silks, medicinal herbs for the Korean court, were purchased.[3]

Through these tributary and trade relations, Ch'ing China

exerted considerable influence on Korean culture. The court ceremonial laws of the Yi dynasty resembled those of Ch'ing China. The court officials were to follow the government regulations concerning the costume code such as colors, woven designs and styles of costumes, as well as the types of hats and insignia. During the middle of the Yi dynasty (16th century), the Korean government ordered that no officials lower than the fifth grade (out of 18 grade ranks of civilian and military officers) could wear any costume made of silk with woven design; silks with woven design were allowed only to fifth-grade and higher government officials and other royal family members. But generally some upper-class members had access to patterned silks. The ladies of the upperclasses preferred wearing expensive Chinese fabrics such as brocade, damask, and embroidered crepe.[4] Embroidered motifs and designs distinguished the ranks of the government officials more sharply than the woven designs.

It is well known that Chinese-Korean arts and textile design are based on symbolism and many books have been written on this topic. Symbolism appears not only on Chinese-Korean silks, but on pottery, porcelain, jade, and other art objects. A wide variety of motifs ranging from Chinese characters, flora, animals, birds, and religious symbols (Buddhist and Taoist) have been used. These symbols were often interpreted differently during the different periods of history.

Chinese-Korean artists not only applied their skill with the intention of merely producing objects pleasing to the eye, but at the same time emblems conveying a definite meaning: the expression of good wishes. To have any adequate appreciation of Chinese-Korean silk design, one must understand the meaning of these symbols and of their relationships one to another.

Chinese-Korean symbolism in silk design can be broadly classified into the expression of man's basic wishes for longevity, happiness, wealth, and numerous progeny. In expressing these basic wishes, Chinese-Korean artists adopted

HUNDRED FORMS OF THE CHARACTER
LONGEVITY 壽

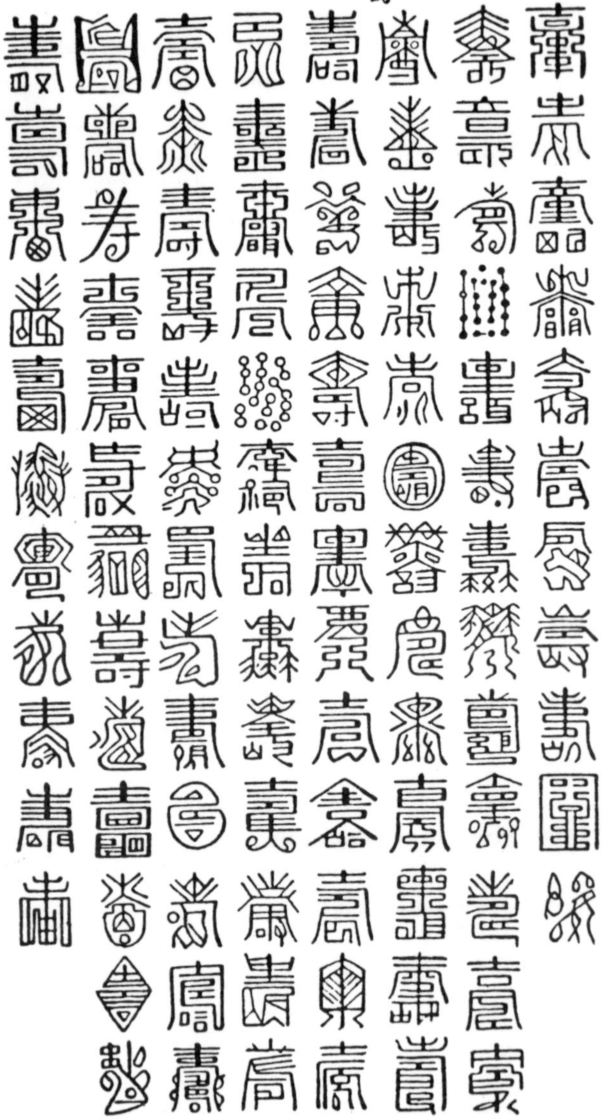

Illustration 1. One hundred forms of the character 'Su' (from Pankala's *Far Eastern Ceramics: Marks and Decoration*, p. 111).

several different means of expression. One way of expressing an idea consists of writing simply the words that indicate it. Chinese letters, with their great elegance and variety of forms, are admirably suited for ornamental use. For instance, the character, 'su'壽, longevity, is one of the most important decorative motifs in ceramics, porcelains, and silk textiles.[5] It may be repeated a hundred times in a hundred different forms (Illustration I).[6] One hundred in such a context simply means many. It commonly appears on woven silk, worked in embroidery, carved in jade, and painted on porcelain, to mention only a few media. Characters, such as 'hŭi'喜, joy; 'pok'福, happiness; and 'pu'富, wealth also appear frequently on Chinese-Korean silks. These characters can be used in various forms: in a square, a seal, grass, and various types of script (Illustrations 2, 3, and 4).

A second means of expression is through a symbol with which there is an association of ideas: thus an ingot of gold represents riches; a book, learning or knowledge; a pomegranate, because of its many seeds, numerous

Chinese Characters	Korean Romanization	Meaning
壽	Su	Longevity
囍	Hŭi	Joy
福	Pok	Happiness
富	Pu	Wealth
萬	Man	Ten Thousand

Illustration 2.
Chinese character motifs which appear frequently on Korean silk design.

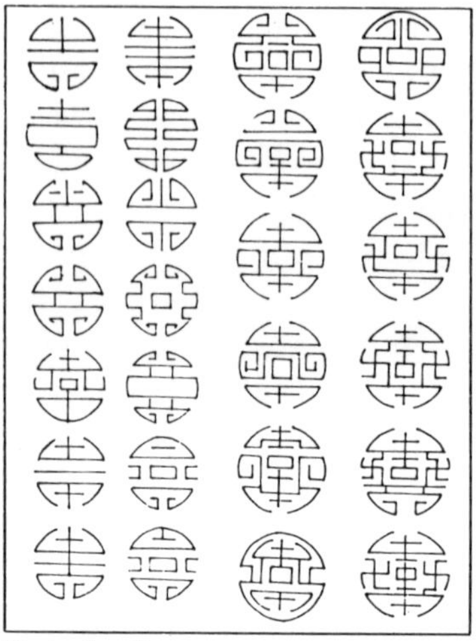

Illustration 3.
The character 'Su' roundels which appear in Korean silk design.

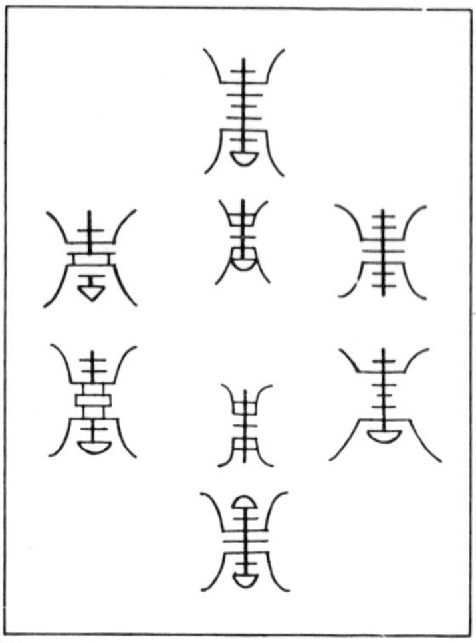

Illustration 4.
The common variation of the character 'Su' in oblong design.

descendents. The crane is believed to live for a thousand years, therefore, represents longevity and is associated with the Taoist idea of immortality.

A third means of expression consists of indicating words by using images that suggest the pronunciations of these words; this being the ordinary device of the rebus. As an example, the procedure of the pun brings us the bat, whose name, 'pok' 蝠 is pronounced like the word, 'pok' 福 which means happiness. Therefore, in order to express wishes for longevity and happiness together, the character, 'su' 壽 is often combined with bat motifs.

Another play upon words is the Buddha hand citron which grows in southern China and has a shape similar to the fingers of a hand. These are called 'pul-su' 佛手 hands of Buddha, and since the 'pul' is similar in sound to the word 'pok,' happiness, this citron has, in the same manner as the bat, become one of the images of happiness.[7]

It is the objective of this study to examine a group of selected Korean traditional silk fabrics woven for dress purpose with regard to these different symbolic expressions.[8] The study will identify the various methods of symbolic expression mentioned above on Korean traditional silks, and decipher the meaning of design produced by the combination of design motifs.

The various methods of expression of symbolism discussed earlier can be summarized as follows:

A. Chinese character.

B. Symbol type I—An image with which there is an association of ideas. Example: pomegranate, numerous descendents.

C. Symbol type II—Substituting words by using images that suggest the pronunciation of these words, this being the ordinary device of rebus. Example: Images of bat are often used in place of 'pok,' happiness.

1. Chinese character and variation (more than one type and/or form of a character).
2. Chinese character plus Symbol Type I and variation (more than one symbol and/or one type or form of a character).
3. Chinese character plus Symbol Type II and variation (more than one symbol and/or one type or form of a character).
4. Chinese character plus Symbol Type I and Symbol Type II and variation (more than one symbol for each type, and/or more than one type or form of a character).
5. Symbol Type I plus Symbol Type II and variation (more than one symbol for each type).
6. Symbol Type I and variation (more than one symbol).
7. Symbol Type II and variation (more than one symbol).

Discussion

Out of seven theoretical possibilities of motif combination, the first four categories include Chinese characters. Among many Chinese characters, the most commonly used characters are 'su,' longevity; 'hŭi,' joy; and 'pok,' happiness.

The common variations of the character 'su' roundel and oblong designs which appear on Korean woven silks are presented in Illustrations 3 and 4. Sometimes swastikas are incorporated into the design of the character (Illustration 3) in which case the wish expressed is increased ten thousand fold, or many times, since the swastika is used by the Chinese and Koreans as a substitute for the character 'man'萬, meaning myriad, ten thousand or simply many (Illustration 2).[9]

1. Chinese Character and Variation (More than one type and/or form of a character).

Figure 1a and 1b illustrate the examples which belong to this category. In Figure 1a, two different configurations of the character 'su' are depicted; one for roundel and another for oblong type. The meaning conveyed is simple, "May you have

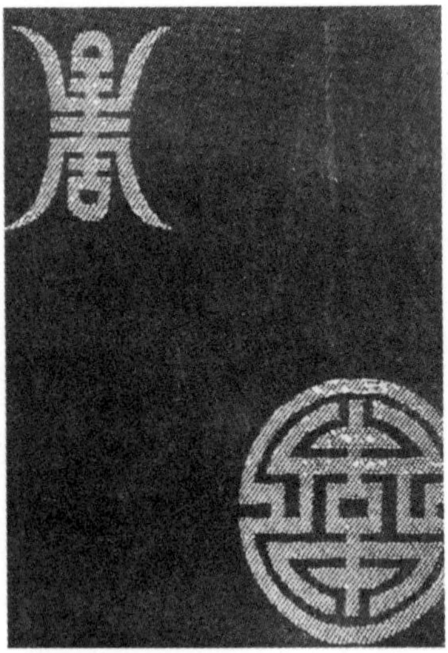

Fig. 1a.
Oblong and roundel types of character 'su' (from the author's collection).

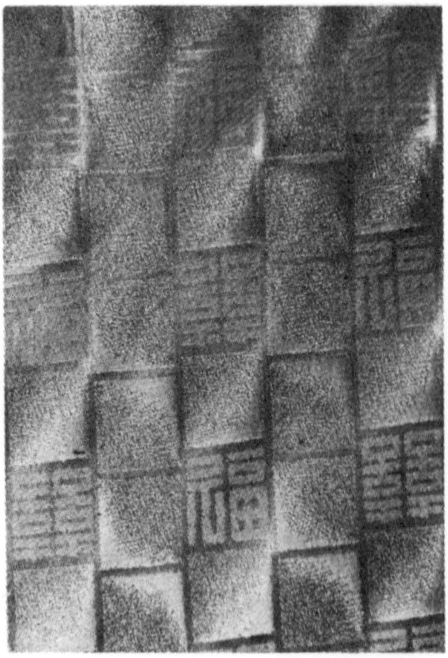

Fig. 1b.
Characters of pok,' happiness, and 'hŭi joy (from the author's collection).

a long life." As a variation under this category, character combination can be used as design motifs. Figure 1b illustrates the combination of character 'hŭi,' joy, and character 'pok,' happiness for design motifs. The meaning conveyed becomes: "May you have a joyful and happy life."

2. Chinese Character Plus Symbol Type I and Variation (More than one symbol and/or one type or form of a character).

Symbol type I is the design motif which has an association of ideas between the motif and the meaning it represents as discussed earlier. In Figure 2a, the character 'hŭi,' joy, is super-imposed with a peony motif, Symbol type I. Peony is regarded in Korea and China as a symbol of riches and nobility. It is also a flower of seasons and stands for spring. It is highly esteemed and was used on princesses' costumes and traditional wedding ceremonial gowns in Korea. The meaning

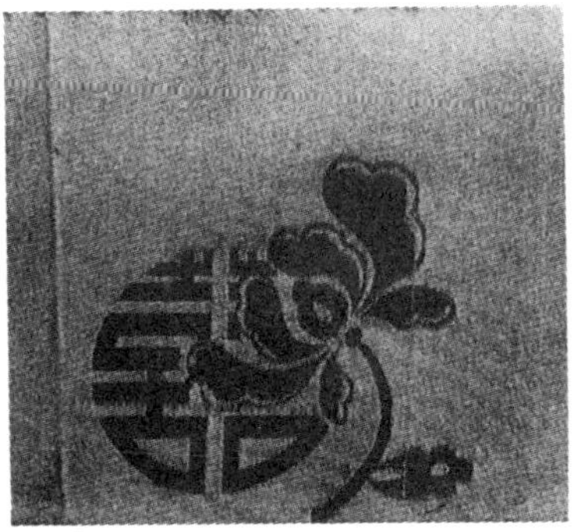

Fig. 2a.
Roundel motif of character 'hŭi,' joy, super-imposed with a stylized peony motif (from the author's collection).

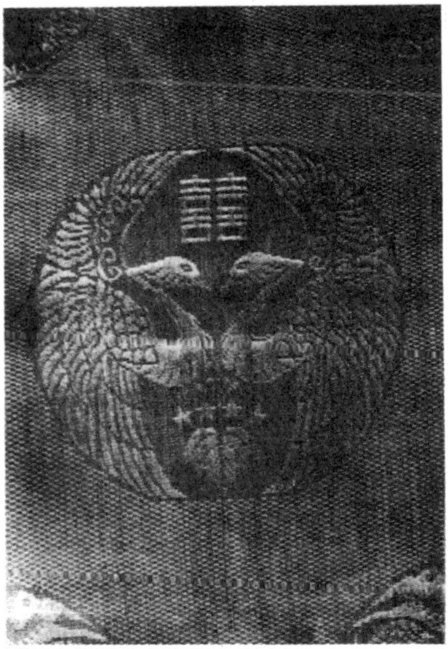

Fig. 2b
A medallion motif composed of two phoenixes (from the author's collection).

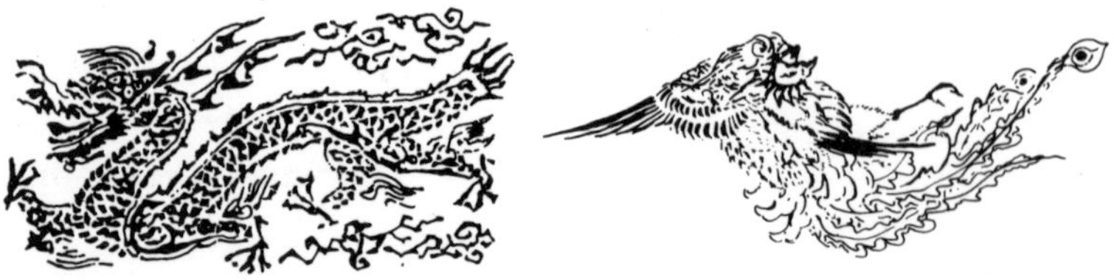

Illustration 5. Dragon and phoenix motifs.

conveyed in Figure 2a is "May you be noble and joyful."

In Figure 2b, the roundel motif is composed of the character 'hŭi,' joy, phoenix, and the paulownia plant. The character, 喜 has the meaning of joy and warmth. It is also the cosmic symbol of the south and influences the summer season.[10] The phoenix, a fabulous suspicious bird, is derived from the Chinese pong-hwang 鳳凰, which was shown in textile designs from ancient days. It is an imaginary bird over six feet high, and its form, half resembling that of a peacock, half that of a pheasant, is like that of the dragon. The phoenix is considered the king of all birds. The male is called pong 鳳 while the female is called hwang 凰. It lives in a forest of paulownia plants and eats only the fruits of bamboo. It is said that this bird never harms or eats live plants or insects. It does not travel or behave indiscreetly. Once it decides to travel, however, no other bird is able to follow it.[11] The phoenix was used as an emblem of the empress, whereas the dragon was the favored emblem of the emperor (Illustration 5).

3. Chinese Character Plus Symbol Type II and Variation (More than one symbol and/or one type or form of a character).

Figure 3a contains the character 'su,' long life and the bat motif, Symbol type II, for the design. The pun of bat is pronounced 'pok' in Korean and it has the same pronunciation as 'pok,' happiness in Chinese character. Therefore, the bat depicts the meaning of happiness using the device of rebus as stated earlier. The bat motif is extensively used in place of the character 'pok,' happiness for Korean silk design. Figure 3b contains the same motifs but in a different arrangement. Five bats surround the character 'su,' longevity, forming a roundel. The five bats depict the five blessings of long live, wealth, to be tranquil or healthy, love of virtue, and natural death.[12] This design motif (character 'su' with five bats) has been widely applied to other art forms such as porcelain, jade, and ceramics in China as well as in Korea.

4. Chinese Character Plus Symbol Type I and Symbol Type II and Variation (More than one symbol for each type and/or more than one type or form of a character).

Figure 4a is similar to Figure 3a in that both contain the character 'su' and the bat motif, Symbol type II, for the design. However, Figure 4a contains the third motif of gourd and its flora, Symbol type I. The gourd denotes numerous descendents and abundance. It also signifies purification or cleanliness due to its capacity to enclose seeds (impurities).[13] In woven designs, the gourd along with garland notes multiple descendents, prosperity, and longevity. The gourd seldom appears alone in woven designs. The total meaning of the design expresses man's basic wishes for longevity (character, 'su'), happiness (bats), and multiple descendents (gourd). In Figure 4b, a simplified version of the character 'su,' five bats (Symbol type II), gourd and cloud (Symbol type I), are included. Cloud, in this case, depicts 'abundance' or 'as great

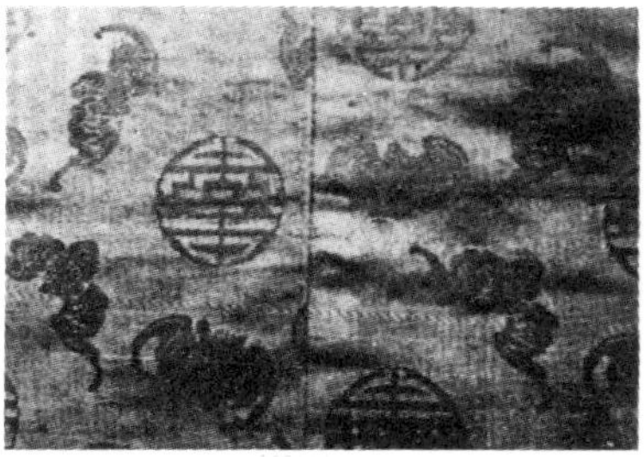

Fig. 3a.
Two motifs of character 'su' and bats (from the Su-Do University Museum).

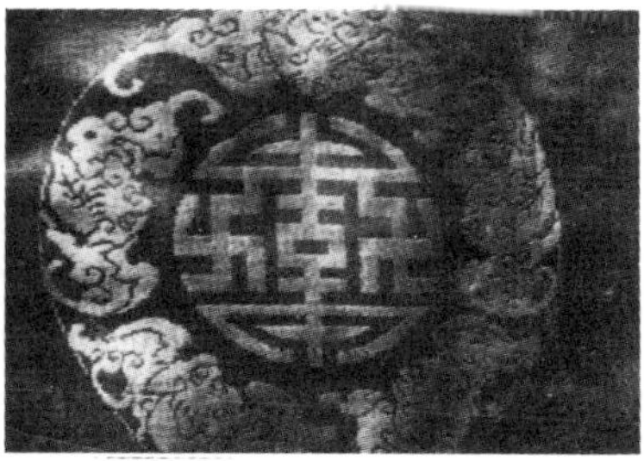

Fig. 3b.
Character 'su,' surrounded by five bats (from the Sŏk Chu Sŏn Collection).

Fig. 4a.
Character 'su' roundels, bats, gourd, and its flora (from the Sŏk Chu Sŏn Collection).

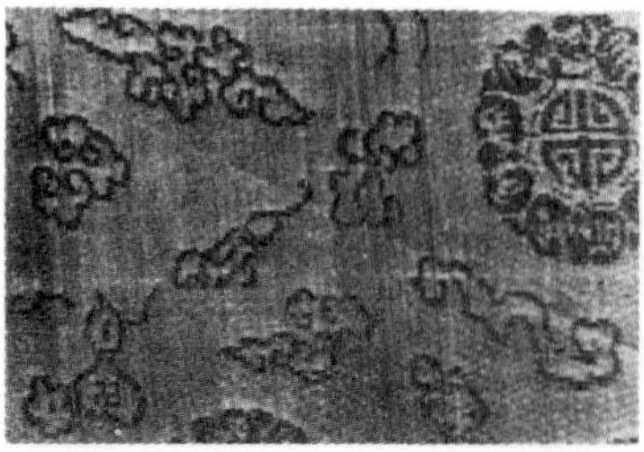

Fig. 4b.
Simplified version of character 'su,' five bats, gourd, and cloud (from the author's collection).

as heaven is high.'[14] Therefore, the total meaning becomes more complex compared with earlier examples. It means, "May you have long life, happiness, multiple descendents all in abundance." As can be seen in this example, the meaning becomes more complex as more motifs are added.

5. Symbol Type Plus Symbol Type II and Variation (More than one symbol for each type).

The three motifs depicted in Figure 5a are the crane, the cloud and the bat. The first two, the crane and the cloud, belong to Symbol type I, meaning crane for longevity, cloud for abundance. The bat means happiness and it is Symbol type II. The total meaning is again, "May you have longevity and happiness as great as heaven is high." Another example is shown in Figure 5b where three different motifs are included in the design. The peach for longevity, the pomegranate for multiple descendents, and Buddha hand citron for happiness of the three thousand worlds of Buddha. The peach and pomegranate are Symbol type I and the Buddha hand citron is Symbol type II. These three fruits are known as Three Sacred Fruits in China and Korea. According to old Chinese mythology, Hsi Wang Mu 西王母(The Queen Mother of the West) owned a peach tree which bore peaches of immortality every thousand years. If one could eat one of these peaches, he might live up to three thousand years.[15] Therefore, the peach has come to symbolize a wish for longevity and is associated with the Taoist idea of immortality. These three symbols are complete in expressing man's three basic wishes for longevity, happiness, and numerous progeny. These three symbols, as a design motif, appear not only on woven designs but also on pottery, ceramics, and other art forms.

6. Symbol Type I and Variation (More than one symbol of this type).

The majority of design motifs of Korean silk design belong to Symbol type I in which there is an association of ideas between the symbol and the meaning. A typical example of this category is floral motif design. In Figure 6a, the lotus motif appears singularly. The lotus represents the evolution of the Buddhistic worlds from the eternal cosmic matter.[16] It is an emblem of purity. Its roots are white as pure jade, and glistening drops of water resting on its spread leaves are symbols of Buddhist enlightenment.[17] There are also abundance of other floral motif designs in Chinese and Korean silks. While flowers of Four Seasons are represented by the tree peony (spring), the lotus (summer), the chrysanthemum (autumn), and the wild plum (winter), the Four Worthies (also called Four Gentlemen) are the prunes blossom, the wild iris (or orchid), the chrysanthemum, and the bamboo. All of these appear singularly or in combination on woven design.

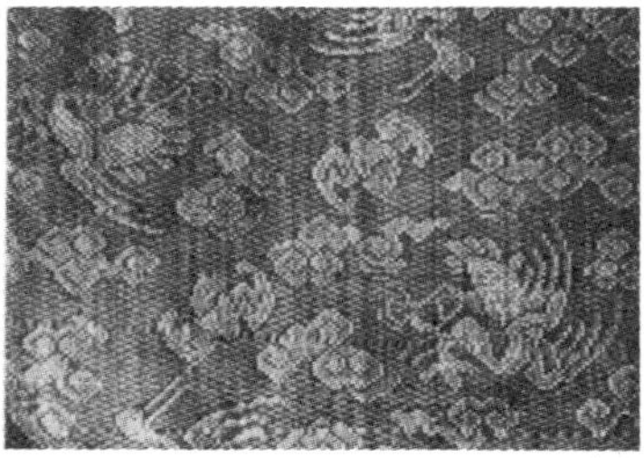

Fig. 5a.
The crane, bat, and the cloud (from the Sŏk Chu Sŏn Collection).

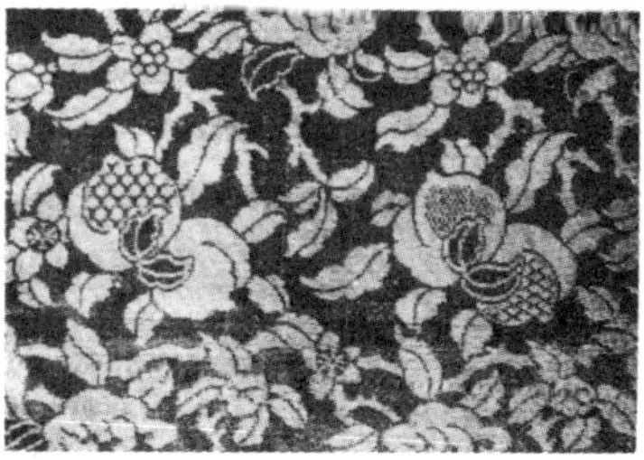

Fig. 5b.
The three Sacred Fruits of peach, Buddha hand citron, and pomegranate (from the Sŏk Chu Sŏn Collection).

Fig. 6a.
Lotus and its flora (from the Sŏk Chu Sŏn Collection).

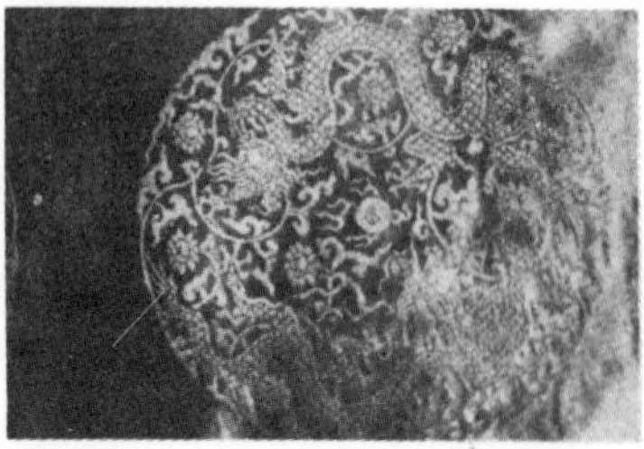

Fig. 6b.
A medallion motif composed of two dragons (from the Su Do University Museum).

Floral designs have a long history in Oriental countries, but it was not until the Sung dynasty that the full manifestation of the floral motif in Chinese art took place. The Sung dynasty was a peaceful era in which artists and poets payed much attention to the natural beauties of flowers and foliage plants. Animal forms still remained but plant forms greatly predominated. Floral motif designs appeared in pottery in great number and artists delighted in painting flowers. From the Sung dynasty down to the Ch'ing or Manchu dynasty, Chinese art has been overwhelmingly floral in its motifs.[18]

Another example of Symbol type I is the dragon. Figure 6b contains a roundel motif in which two dragons are facing each other in opposite directions. The dragons are surrounded by vines, flora, and cloud motifs. The pearl or the ball is in the middle of the roundel. The dragon represents excellence. The dragon, often seen with a ball or a pearl, presides over the water and rain. In times of drought, it is invoked in the hope that abundant rain will come and save the crops. Therefore, it is natural that to an agricultural people such as the Chinese and Koreans, the dragon 龍, bringer of fertility to the fields, became the symbol of whatever is most powerful and best in the world.[19] In the sixth century A.D., it assumed what, thereafter, became its predominant shape, with a camel's head, stag's antlers, serpent's body, and four feet armed with claws. In relatively recent periods, the dragon became the emblem of the emperor, who alone had the privilege of using the ornamentation of robes, banners, and utensils, the motif of a dragon with five claws. Lesser princes could also use a dragon design, but with only three or four claws.[20] One of the commonest motifs is the dragons soaring above the Taoist Isles of the Blest or above Mt. Meru, which belongs to the Buddhist cycle of ideas. They are surrounded by clouds and flames, and before them floats a pearl which may be more correctly interpreted as a Buddhist jewel than as the solar disk.[21] Dragons are depicted on the emperor's costumes, Buddhist monk's robes, and Taoist priest's robes (Illustration 5).

7. Symbol Type II and Variation (More than one symbol of this type).

There are no examples which belong to this category. Symbol type II is the design motif of which the pronunciation is the same as some other words. An example is the bat whose pronunciation is the same as that of happiness. Another example is the Buddha hand citron whose pronunciation is similar to that of happiness. None of these motifs are depicted singularly in any Korean silk design.

Summary

All of these different methods of symbolic expression have appeared on the silk fabrics of the court costumes and those of the noble class of Korea. Modern traditional Korean costumes still contain most of these motifs and various methods of symbolic expression with a higher degree of elegance and a greater variety of colors than the costumes of earlier periods, and they are enjoyed by everybody in Korean society.

NOTES

1. Chŏn, Hae-jong, "Sino-Korean Tributary Relations in the Ch'ing Period," *The Chinese World Order,* ed. John King Fairbank (Cambridge: Harvard University Press, 1968), p. 90.
2. *Ibid.*
3. *Ibid.* p. 107.
4. Ch'oe, Ok-cha, *A Study of Colors and Patterns Based on Actual Objects, Chiefly Concerned with Clothes in the Days of the Yi Dynasty* (Seoul: Su-Do University Press, 1972), p. 16.
5. All Chinese characters in this study are romanized in Korean.
6. Maria Penkala, *Far Eastern Ceramics: Marks and Decorations* (Netherlands: Mouton and Company, 1963), p. 111.
7. Edouard Chavannes, *Five Happiness: Symbolism in Chinese Popular Art* (New York: Weatherhill, 1973), p. 21.
8. Kwŏn (Suk) Yun-hŭi, Symbolic and Decorative Function of Motifs in Korean Woven Silk Design: 1875-1975 (Doctoral Dissertation, University of Wisconsin, 1977).
9. Chavannes, *ibid,* p. 39.
10. Michael Sullivan, *The Arts of China* (Berkeley: University of California Press, 1973), p. 83.
11. Sŏk, Chu-sŏn, Traditional Korean Textile Motifs—Lecture Series to Ladies, Tae-Han Ilbo (Korean Daily Newspaper), Seoul, 2–16 March, 1973.
12. Judith and Arthur H. Burling. *Chinese Art* (New York: Bonanza Books, 1953), p. 351.
13. Suk.
14. Katherine Ball, *Decorative Motives of Oriental Art* (London: John Lane, The Bodley Head, 1927), p. 259.
15. C. A. S. Williams, *Encyclopedia of Chinese Symbolisms and Art Motives* (New York: The Julian Press, 1960), p. 312.
16. Stanley C. Nott, *Chinese Jade throughout the Ages* (Tokyo: Charles E. Tuttle Co., 1962), p. 132.
17. *Ibid.*
18. Arthur de Carlo Sowervy, *Nature in Chinese Art* (New York: John Day Co., 1940), p. 131.
19. Chavannes, *ibid,* p. 18.
20. *Ibid.*, p. 79.
21. Martin Feddersen, *Chinese Decorative Art* (New York: Thomas Yoseloff, 1961), p. 235.

Contributors in This volume

Kim Wŏn-yong	Professor of Archaeology, Seoul National University, and Curator of the University Museum
Chin Hong-sŏp	Professor of Korean Art History, Ewha Womans University, Seoul, and Curator of the University Museum
Hwang Su-yŏng	Professor, Dongguk University, Seoul
An Kye-hyŏn	Professor An, deceased, was Professor of Buddhist Studies, Dongguk University
Ch'oe Sun-u	Director, National Museum of Korea
Chŏng Yang-mo	A former Curator at the National Museum of Korea, Kyŏngju
Sin Yŏng-hun	Secretary, Korean Folklorist Society
Kwŏn Yun-hŭi	Assistant Professor of Home Economics, Northern Illinois University, USA